New Zealand National Parks

Page 1 **The lush greens of a beech forest, Mt Aspiring National Park.**
This page **Aoraki/Mount Cook, Mount Cook National Park.**
Pages 4–5 **Franz Josef Glacier, Westland National Park.**
Page 6 **Morning fog above Lake Matheson, with Mount Tasman and**
Aoraki/Mount Cook reflected in its quiet waters, Westland National Park.

Published 2006 by David Bateman Ltd,
30 Tarndale Grove, Albany, Auckland, New Zealand

ISBN-13: 978-1-86953-594-0
ISBN-10: 1-86953-594-4

Editorial services Jeanette Cook
Design Trevor Newman
Photograph on page 66 supplied by Graeme Matthews
Map Russell Kirkpatrick/MediaMerge Mapping
Printed in China through Colorcraft Ltd, Hong Kong

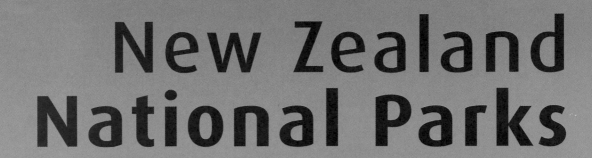

New Zealand National Parks

Photographs David Muench

Editor Kennedy Warne

David Bateman

Contents

Introduction

Natural high Kennedy Warne

It's New Year's Eve and I am intoxicated, but not in the usual sense. This is a natural high—a sensory cocktail brought about by walking four hours into a New Zealand forest. The sights, sounds and smells I'm drinking in are as heady as a glass of champagne. Best of all, I'm enjoying them with my 20-year-old daughter, who has spurned more conventional revelling in favour of spending the 31st of December on a mountain with her father. She wants to greet the new year in the presence of nature, far from the madding crowd.

So here we are in Egmont National Park on the last day of 2005, making for Lake Dive Hut, racing the setting sun. Overhead, the forest canopy is being shaken and stirred by 30-knot (55.5 km/h) winds. The trees creak and groan as if holding a conversation. But on the forest floor there is barely enough breeze to shiver the ferns or ruffle the mosses that hang from every branch like dwarves' beards.

We stop beside a tree fuchsia and finger its papery orange bark, which peels from the trunk as the tree grows and mounds up at the base. I remind Emily that she once wrote a letter to her mother on a piece of this bark. We are hoping to climb to the summit of Egmont/Taranaki, the mountain around which the park was created over a century ago, but the forecast is for the high winds to persist, so a summit attempt may not be possible. Not to worry; this national park has more than enough forest trails to keep us occupied for the few days we are here.

We press on, the track dipping and climbing, narrowing and widening, as variable as a river. In some places vegetation almost reaches across the path, and you walk as if pushing through the swing doors of a pub. But you have to take care which plants you push aside. The snaking tendrils of bush lawyer have sharp hooks that snag cruelly on clothing and skin.

It's almost too dark to see, but neither of us wants to be the first to turn on a torch. It's a pride thing. So we pretend to have bionic vision and keep walking, willing the hut to appear.

At last it shows itself. Remarkably, it's deserted. I can't believe that we're the only people who have chosen to spend New Year's Eve in the splendid isolation of this lovely place. By the dancing light of our head-torches we perform the familiar rituals of hut cooking, ferreting in our packs for ingredients and utensils, then trying to create a little culinary magic over a tiny gas burner. As we wait for the food to cook I catch my daughter's eye and ask the rhetorical question that has become our catchphrase in the outdoors: 'Does it get any better than this?'

We both know the answer. It is one for which we can thank the progenitors of New Zealand's national park system—pioneer sportsmen and conservationists whose efforts, spanning more than a century, have resulted in the fourteen national parks we have today.

These parks—from Tongariro, created in 1887, to Rakiura, created in 2002—form the heart of what is referred to as the conservation estate, the nearly 8 million hectares (19.7 million acres)—a third of New Zealand's land area—that is set aside as parks and reserves for the preservation of landscapes and species. And, many would add, for the preservation of their own sanity. It is in natural spaces like these—which New Zealanders affectionately call 'the great outdoors'—that so many of us find refreshment and renewal.

For me, the species aspect has always been important. Whether I have been looking for cave spiders or moa skeletons, alpine grasshoppers or flightless swamphens, national parks have been the location. These protected areas—and predator-free sanctuaries within them—hold much of what remains of New Zealand's indigenous biodiversity. To experience the creaturely profusion that exists in a wildlife sanctuary is to glimpse this country's biota as it was before human impact; before the ecological blitzkrieg brought about by fire and hunting and the introduction of mammalian predators.

Right **Mount Ruapehu** and tussock grasses from along the upper Taranaki Falls track, Tongariro National Park.

Night is a good time to go looking. Once, in the Murchison Mountains of Fiordland, a naturalist friend decided to conduct an impromptu nocturnal survey of the local invertebrate life. We set ourselves the additional challenge of finding as many green creatures as we could. In a place as prodigiously green as Fiordland, we expected that many of the residents would have sought safety in camouflage.

By lantern beam and flashlight, we scanned the moss-covered trunks of the forest trees. Native cockroaches, gleaming like varnished mahogany, paused, antennae twitching. Shiny black pill bugs rolled into balls but did not fall from their mossy perches. Spiders stood guard over crevices in the bark—perfect websites. But nothing green so far. We ran the lantern beam along fallen logs, marvelling at the forest in miniature: coconut-palm mosses towering above crumpled crusts of salmon and lime lichen; beech seedlings sprouting among filmy ferns; fungal spores held aloft on spires and nestled in bright orange cups. In a place as monumental as Fiordland, which occupies over a million hectares (2.5 million acres) of the South Island, the beauty of this microcosm was doubly breathtaking. A crane fly—a gangly-legged insect that looks like an overgrown mosquito—careered into the lantern, then flitted away. I made a wild swing and caught it. Aha! Its body was a ghostly shade of green. Minutes later we found a green harvestman, looking like a ladybug on stilts, and then a green crab spider. Just after midnight we heard a kiwi—a shrill, rising cry with a guttural screech at the end, repeated a dozen or more times. Silence. Then a second call, strong and challenging, from across the valley. 'Males staking out their territories,' whispered my friend above the hiss of the lantern. Maori call this species of kiwi 'tokoeka', 'bird with a walking stick'—an apt description of New Zealand's long-beaked national symbol. Even in national parks as large and remote as Fiordland, kiwi have become scarce. There are no fences around these special areas, and isolation has not held the rising tide of introduced predators at bay.

The beauty of New Zealand's national-park network is not just that it preserves a sizable slice of the country in perpetuity but that it provides access for would-be visitors in the form of tracks and huts.

When the river is rising or the snow falling, and darkness is closing in, there's no place on earth like a tramping hut. They range from bare-bones shelters to swanky lodges that sleep 60, and national parks wouldn't be the same without them. Some approach the status of historic places. I visited one venerable shelter—Sefton Bivvy in Mt Cook National Park—with Derek Grzelewski, whose essays introduce four of the parks featured in this book. Sefton Bivvy is at the dog-kennel end of the size spectrum. Erected in 1917 on a spur below The Footstool, it is a corrugated-iron A-frame that is not quite high enough for a person to stand upright inside. Rocks are stacked to waist height against its orange walls to stop the hut being blown away.

This is not just a hypothetical threat, Derek assured me. In 1977, gale-force winds lifted a hut off its foundations and pitched it into a ravine, killing its occupants. I thought about those unfortunate climbers as I tried to sleep that night. The wind slapped at the hut, graunching the sheets of iron against the nails that held them. Icy draughts sneaked past the scrunched-up newspapers climbers had stuffed into cracks in the walls. We brewed soup and tea and dozed to the howl of the wind and the distant crack of falling rocks. It was good to have a roof over our heads.

The most distinctive hut I ever stayed in was the 'Doughboy Hilton', which sprawls in Heath Robinson quirkiness behind the sand dunes of Doughboy Bay, on Rakiura's west coast. It started life as a tiny Forest Service A-frame, but generations of hunters and trampers have done a DIY job on it, extending it with generous amounts of plywood and polythene so that it sleeps eight comfortably.

My daughter and I were on a kiwi-spotting trip. We had flown in to Doughboy Bay, landing on the beach, and would tramp north to Mason Bay and fly out a couple of days later. This part of Stewart Island is renowned for kiwi, which can be seen during the day, not just at night.

One of the pleasures of a tramping trip is the moment when you push open the door of a hut for the

Above Knobs Flat alongside the Eglinton River, Fiordland National Park.

first time and look around your new temporary dwelling. The Doughboy Hilton was clearly the work of experienced back-country decorators. Lengths of fishing net served as hammock-style mattresses. There was a potbelly stove for heating and cooking; chopped wood was stored under the beds. The kitchen had a rat-proof safe (full of army rations when we visited) and shelves of pots and pans (even a wok), fishing lines and other paraphernalia. A home away from home.

Outside, plastic buoys hung from overhanging branches and a guttering system channelled rainwater into tanks. There was an outdoor eating area under a tarpaulin. The skull of a pilot whale lay on the table.

That night, we cooked pasta on the potbelly stove and baked damper in the firebox on supplejack twigs. Then, with the cool sand squeezing between our toes, we stalked kiwi through the dunes.

Huts on many of the most popular hiking routes have wardens during summer. Once, when walking the Greenstone Trail between Fiordland and Lake Wakatipu, I met an unforgettable character who had set up his hut as a kind of hippy kingdom. When I arrived, Michel and his girlfriend, Oli, were sunbathing on the deck to rock music from a ghetto blaster hooked up to a solar panel. Oli had just baked a batch of sticky coconut muffins. Michel brought a flagon of bush beer out of the fridge, and we spent the afternoon in feasting, languid conversation and games of hacky sack. Next day, it took some self-discipline to shoulder my pack and leave this comfortable oasis.

Wherever I tramp, I'm curious to know who has trod the path before me. What did they see? How did they respond? Hut books are wonderful repositories of tramping experience, connecting you to the community of fellow travellers. Often a hut entry is a terse few words about the state of the track, the weather, the hunting ('Saw 5 deer, shot 0'), the insect life ('I hate sandflies'). Sometimes a bit of homespun philosophy is offered. Occasionally a few lines of doggerel, like these, written in a Fiordland hut during an especially patience-testing stretch of bad weather:

> *It rained and rained and rained—*
> *The average fall was well maintained.*
> *And when the tracks were simply bogs*
> *It started raining cats and dogs.*
> *After a drought of half an hour*
> *We had a most refreshing shower,*
> *And then the most curious thing of all:*
> *A gentle rain began to fall.*
> *Next day also was fairly dry,*
> *Save for a deluge from the sky,*
> *Which wetted the party to the skin,*
> *And after that—the rain set in!*

History can add a pleasing grace note to a wilderness journey, or be the reason for making it. As he writes in his essay on Kahurangi National Park, Gerard Hindmarsh sought to follow in the footsteps—or, more precisely, the toe- and finger-holds—of a pioneer surveyor who made a precarious coastal trek. In his reflections on Rakiura, Carl Walrond ponders the lonely labours of farmers at Mason Bay, and the hermit-like existence of a Japanese woman who lived in a cave at Doughboy Bay. Derek Grzelewski chases the ghost of 'Mr Explorer' Douglas, eternally wandering the Westland hills.

In most cases, one's predecessors on the trail have left no greater mark than their bootprints, or perhaps a makeshift cairn to mark a river crossing. But New Zealand's national parks are not without larger artefacts, none stranger than the relics of the Stewart Island 'tin rush'—a nineteenth-century stampede of prospectors

Right A forest interior of mosses and ferns reflected in a stream along Minnehaha walk at Fox Glacier, Westland National Park.

into the inhospitable weather and impenetrable scrub around Port Pegasus in the hope of striking it rich. A vain hope, it turned out—the size of the tin lode had been hyped to high heaven, and most miners got nought for their efforts. To see the rusting water pipes and valves of that doomed enterprise lying among the fern and moss of the regenerating bush is to be transported back to that time of dreams, when the next shovelful of dirt could unearth a bonanza.

I visited the Tin Range as part of a week-long kayaking trip around Port Pegasus, a harbour so large that an early surveyor declared it had anchoring room 'for all the ships in the British dominions'. On a day too stormy for paddling, my companions and I took a rough track that led to the old tin workings. For a couple of kilometres the track followed a wooden tramway, built by miners to shift sluicing equipment. Dozens of neat, round holes in softer parts of the soil puzzled us until we realised they had been made by the bills of kiwi probing for grubs and worms.

The wind on the ridge was ferocious. We could barely stand upright as we picked our way around thickets of leatherwood and granite pillars that loomed like weird sculptures through the swirling cloud. Rain, accelerated by the wind, peppered our faces like buckshot until the skin was raw.

We found a tunnel that miners had driven 85 m (279 ft) into the granite heart of the range. As we waded down the flooded drive, torches in hand, we could see the indentations left by the miners' pick-axes in the walls. The rock sparkled with mica and quartz. At the end was a hole drilled for a dynamite charge that was never made. Reality had finally prevailed, and the project was abandoned.

Kayaking is a fine way to experience national parks that border the sea. Parts of Fiordland, Kahurangi and Rakiura are readily accessible by kayak, and Abel Tasman is now almost as famous for its paddling opportunities as for its coastal tramping. Where the bush is thick and tracks are few, as around Port Pegasus, paddling affords access to beauty spots denied the landlubber. To reach Smugglers Cove, for instance, we slipped through a slot in the rocks not much wider than our paddles and found a jewel of a bay shaded by forest down to the water's edge. At one point in our journey the sea was full of jellyfish, and every few paddle strokes there would be a soft thud as paddle hit jelly. A sea lion followed us up an estuary to our camp beneath Bald Cone, one of several eroded granite domes that protrude through the forest like grey thimbles. At dawn we climbed the peak and listened to the cries of sea and forest birds. To the west lay biblically named Gog and Magog, the highest peaks on this part of the island.

Later, in sparkling sunshine, we paddled down a narrow arm of Port Pegasus, dragged our boats ashore and crossed a narrow neck of land to Broad Bay, the southernmost beach in New Zealand. Beyond its dazzling sands, fine as flour, lay the Southern Ocean. We carved a ball from a kelp stalk and played a game of cricket, then pitched our tents and built a driftwood fire. At dusk we watched yellow-eyed penguins come ashore, surfing in on the breakers and marching up the beach to their roosts in the scrub. We drank coffee and talked around the fire as faint streaks of aurora tinted the sky. As the night grew darker, flecks of green appeared in the sand; the beach was alive with phosphorescent sandhoppers. Held up to torchlight they looked like ordinary sandhoppers, a nondescript cream colour, yet in the dark they shone like specks of Kryptonite. None of us had ever seen anything like it.

Such moments are, for me, the essence of the national-park experience. They happen far from the beaten track, involve the companionship of others and reveal nature's endless capacity to surprise. They remind me of Theodore Roosevelt's dictum, chiselled in stone in the great entry hall of the American Museum of Natural History: 'There are no words that can tell the hidden spirit of the wilderness; that can reveal its mystery, its melancholy and its charm.' That hidden spirit is the subject of this book. In pictures and words, their limitations notwithstanding, these pages celebrate that vital mystery—the spell of the wild.

Above A window in the rock on Bald Cone frames granite domes around Port Pegasus, on the southern tip of Stewart Island, Rakiura National Park.

Despite a bruised and battered past, tiny Abel Tasman has emerged as a jewel among New Zealand's national parks—and a place to experience biological giants.

Abel Tasman National Park
I brake for snails Gerard Hindmarsh

The tumble of little mountains that juts out into the sea to separate Tasman and Golden Bays at the northern tip of the South Island is far from pristine. Its coastal hillsides of depleted soils are in some places overrun with introduced weeds and its hinterland has none of the mirror lakes, crunching glaciers and towering icons of rock and ice that are the pride of other parks.

Compared to the country's thirteen other national parks, this place is tiny, just 22,530 ha (55,630 acres) as against Fiordland's *massive* 1.26 million (3.1 million). It is tempting to say that the Abel Tasman is barely big enough to get lost in, were it not for the fact that hardened trampers and pig-hunters who venture into its interior will vouch for some of the most steeply inaccessible and confusing terrain to be found anywhere.

So how does New Zealand's smallest national park come to rate so high in the public's estimation? In 2005 some 160,000 visitors took in the Abel Tasman, making it the most intensely visited park in the country. Many of those people would have come away regarding this idyllic meeting of land and sea as the closest thing they had experienced to heaven on earth, a piece of coastal paradise up there among the world's special places when it comes to evoking sentiment.

Seeing is believing. Opalescent waters, sweeping sandy beaches, picture-postcard inlets, granite stacks, frolicking seals and pretty offshore islets set in a normally sparkling sea all combine to thoroughly enchant. Pioneer surveyor Frederick Carrington wrote in 1841, 'I just cannot adequately describe the beauty of the little nooks along this section of coast.'

Today those hiking along the 50-km (31-mile) Coast Track must still subject themselves to scene after scene of unutterable beauty. They do so largely without the weather worries that plague visitors to other, more 'extreme' parks. Lying in the lee of Nelson's ranges, the Abel Tasman enjoys a benevolent climate, with much of its coastline protected from savage westerly and southerly winds.

Travellers must still prepare for wet and chilly weather, and sea kayakers need to be ready for the stiff afternoon winds that spring up off exposed headlands. I say this from experience. I still swear that squall came out of nowhere. It seemed to take just seconds for the slight sea swell I had been delighting in to be transformed into a confusion of seething whitecaps.

With full rudder and furious paddling I managed to turn my kayak around to face into the wind, at the same time taking in my extremely vulnerable position. Less than 50 m (164 ft) astern loomed the granite rocks of Awaroa Head, where a safe landing would have been impossible. I had to find shelter, and fast. Canoe Bay would do, if I could make it.

I mustered my courage and dug the paddle into slush-cake waves. The sting of salt spray up my nose is a feeling I will never forget. Three times I nearly capsized in that sloppy sideways sea, saving myself each time with a massive lunge into the underbelly of a wave. My arms ached, but I was making headway. I cleared the

Right **Totaranui Stream** inlet and headlands.

big rocks, then the smaller boulders, and, with a final rush of adrenaline, took my boat into the surging surf, making it halfway to shore before skewing sideways and going over.

I came up spluttering but relieved to find I was in chest-deep water. I hauled my kayak up the sandy rise and collapsed on it—temporarily stranded, but hardly marooned. Exactly one hour later I flagged down a passing water-taxi and was carted, kayak and all, back to Awaroa Bay, where I admit to having felt a little humbler than when I had set out.

For the Abel Tasman's land-bound visitors it is the tides, rather than the winds, that command special attention. All activity along this coast abides by the rise and fall of the sea. Sometimes you just have to wait a couple of hours for that tidal crossing, or take the alternative track around an inlet like the one at Torrent Bay. Count it as a blessing, for you might otherwise miss the side trip to such gems as Cleopatra's Pool.

Each of these inlets has a distinct personality. Maori called the intimate lagoon at Bark Bay 'Wairima', meaning five streams, after the delightful mossy watercourses that run into it. After you negotiate the sandspit here, the low-tide crossing is not much more than a hop, step and a jump.

Quite different is the traverse across expansive Awaroa Inlet. From the isolated road end that runs into the inlet's north-west corner, you have no option but to engage an expanse of sticky mud scattered with shells, then to ford the river before reaching the far side by the airstrip, exactly 3 km (nearly 2 miles) from where you started. Even the direct kilometre-wide crossing between Awaroa Hut and Pound Creek can leave one feeling exposed and puny at the thought of the terrific tidal force that floods in here twice a day. These tidal fluctuations would have been well known to Maori, who established permanent settlements and temporary camps all along the Abel Tasman coast. Archaeologists have discovered the remains of kumara storage pits, hut terraces, defensive ditches, middens and cemetery sites. The argillite stone tools found at these sites, however, were imported—fashioned from blanks quarried at d'Urville Island and up the Matai River, near Nelson.

The park is named for Dutch explorer and trader Abel Janzoon Tasman, who will always be remembered for his provocative first contact with Maori in 1642 somewhere west of Separation Point—a bizarre exercise in cross-cultural miscommunication which left four of his crew dead. However, it was the French navigator Dumont d'Urville, almost two centuries later, who left the greater legacy. D'Urville explored and charted this coastline in his corvette *Astrolabe* in 1827. Not only did he earn the trust of local Maori, but he left behind place names that give the southern part of the park a French flavour: Coquille, Guilbert, Jules, Adolphe, Simonet, Lesson and Torrent Bay. And, to honour his wife, Adele Island.

Later, zealous Victorian settlers fell upon this coastline with conquering intent, using bullock teams and rough-built tramways to haul out the millable logs, burning off the bush to sow pastures of ryegrass, and building utopian homesteads in all but the most beautiful bays.

Some dynasties left indelible associations: the Huffams of Bark Bay, the Hadfields of Awaroa, the Handcocks of Wharawharangi and the Gibbs of Totaranui. Grandiose William Gibbs typified this generation of little empire builders. After purchasing Totaranui in 1855, he rid the swampy flat of its towering matai, miro, rimu, kahikatea and pukatea trees, then proceeded to plant an avenue of planes and macrocarpas. From the 'landing stage'—his curious term for the beach—he would collect his sea-borne guests in a small carriage pulled by a cream pony and convey them via the avenue to his mansion, which was surrounded by lawns and flower beds. That original homestead burned down in 1930, but Gibbs' plantings still preside over the family campground and centre for park activities that exist on the site today.

But if the logging and burning of coastal forest became common practice, the expected prosperity did not last long. The timber trees soon ran out, and the poor granite soils did not yield anywhere near what the graziers expected. One by one the fine houses were abandoned, and a ragged tide of fern crept over the former farmlands. Wilding pines and gorse invaded to swathe entire hillsides, while around Tonga and Awaroa

Above Marahau River inlet and Sandy Bay.

repeated burn-offs made the impoverished country susceptible to the advance of dreaded spiny hakea—a noxious Australian shrub in the protea family. More lighted matches seemed to be the only remedy, and the sight from out at sea in the 1930s would have made any modern conservationist weep; about three-quarters of the coastal landscape was blackened and scarred by continual burning.

A few small forest reserves did manage to escape axe and flame. But it took the advocacy of Perrine Moncrieff, of Nelson, and other far-sighted individuals to convince the government to combine these protected pieces with purchases of large tracts of private land and finally declare a national park in December 1942, 300 years after Commander Tasman's fateful encounter. The buy-up was not across the board, however, and hikers are often surprised to find themselves walking beside the sizeable enclaves of private land that still exist, in particular at Torrent Bay and Awaroa, with their near-suburban ambience.

Environmentally, Abel Tasman National Park has been called a 'giant experiment in landscape recovery'. Apart from a little help in the form of the concerted felling of wilding pines and the odd amenity planting, it is little more than the natural cycle of regrowth at work. Old pasture is smothered out by fern, which is then invaded by gorse and kanuka. Out of this fine nursery sprout broad-leafed shrubs, which in turn become the understorey for taller tree species, and the cycle back to indigenous forest nears completion.

The recovery process is by no means universal. A short diversion up the confused jumble of rocks that makes up the bed of the Falls River can give the coastal hiker some idea of the terrain lying in the park's interior. From Astrolabe Roadstead, a branch track ventures up to Castle Rocks through what d'Urville described as 'gloomy, sterile deserts', where in places even mosses and lichens find it hard to grow. At higher altitude the granite bedrock of the park is replaced by a belt of ancient marble and limestone, a brooding landscape that rainwater has etched into a bizarre pattern of rifts, rills, runnels and flutings. Faint boomings can often be heard coming from the coast, where the sea pounds the granite cliffs.

As with all karst landscapes, the most spectacular features lie underground. Just outside the park, down a track from Canaan, off the Takaka Hill Road between Nelson and Golden Bay, is Harwood's Hole, the largest vertical shaft in the country at 176 m (577 ft) deep, which offers cavers an awesome plunge into the void. The first spelunkers to venture down this giant geological throat did so in 1957—though a member of that party was killed by a rock dislodged from the top while he was being winched back up. Cavers later blasted out a narrow neck in calcite-sparkling Starlight Cave, which drains the Hole, to avoid having to make the return ascent.

From the Canaan plateau and adjoining Moa Park area, three forest routes descend to the lower reaches of Golden Bay. The graded Rameka Track was the first packhorse-capable path put in over the Pikikuruna Range down to the Takaka valley. Today it is a favourite with a newer breed of riders: recreational mountain-bikers. Some may have the privilege, as I did, of skidding to a halt beside one of the hamburger-sized *Powelliphanta* snails that frequent these slopes. Like a pedestrian crossing the road, it had emerged from its hiding place after rain, its huge grey-marbled foot slick with mucus as it methodically probed left and right, extending its feelers in search of prey. These mahogany-shelled giants of the snail world are as precious as kiwi and tuatara.

There are other giants hereabouts. Dropping into the forested upper valley reaches of the Wainui River, the Wainui Track passes through stands of huge buttressed red beech trees, many with trunks 30 m (98 ft) high and nearly 2 m (6 ft 6 in) in diameter. The furrowed bark of these ancient giants is festooned with all manner of mosses and lichens, but the crowns and lower branches are largely free of epiphytic plants, leaving the millions of little leaves to glow translucent in the sunlight. Only the dedicated hiker gets to see this matchless canopy. Day trippers typically saunter up from Wainui Bay, through groves of black mamaku, wheki tree ferns and nikau, to ogle at the dramatic cascade of Wainui Falls; but they rarely push on past this point, and therefore miss the summer-flowering northern rata and the dramatic splashes of red it adds to the forest vista.

As always, the spoils are to the keen. Abel Tasman may be small, but it offers giant rewards.

Left Rocky headlands along Anapai Bay.

Far right **Totaranui** sand ripples.
Right **Low tide in Sandy Bay.**
Below **Ballon Rock** silhouetted against the dawn light on Torrent Bay.

Left The brilliant blues of Torrent Bay.
Right Understorey in coastal forest
along the Anapai Bay Track.
Below Arch windows in granite
looking through to Tinline Bay.

Mountainous Arthur's Pass National Park, the South Island's first national park, is bisected by the historic road between Canterbury and the West Coast, a connection maintained by a hardy breed of road builders who endure all that the harsh alpine environment can throw at them.

Arthur's Pass National Park
A road among the mountains Mark Scott

There was a moment there in Arthur's Pass when I saw myself abandoning Auckland. I'd seen the road-builders chiselling, hacking and hewing at raw rock under spotlight at midnight, with sleet roaring and swirling off the cliffside into an alpine void. At the bar I'd heard nonchalant tales of avalanche and rockfall and the rumble of earthquakes. I'd smelled lightning in the air.

I wanted to be part of it. I wanted to build a road among mountains. I'd find a cabin in the woods. Sign on. Take my place on the jackhammer at the edge. Join that heroic labour. Become part of an unsung and noble gang of workers that for more than a hundred years has pioneered this country.

Up here, nothing has changed. In 1866, archdeacon Henry Harper wrote of the pass: 'It is sterile, bleak and savage enough to be the haunt of Kuhleborn himself, with attendant gnomes and sprites, for it's flanked by majestic precipices of rock scored with channels, down which the watergod comes in great cascades.' And, I can add, bedevilled by electric storms the like of which only a mountain dweller knows. On one such night, I sat pressing my nose against the frozen glass of the chalet window, a duvet wrapped around my shoulders, while for hours on end the valley, the surrounding peaks, the entire snowclad world was caught in repeated flashbulb glare, followed in an instant by thunder of explosive volcanic force. A kind of concussive crashing that seemed to grow from the very foundations of the mountains.

Over breakfast at the guesthouse, with the beeches still tossing their heads in a tantrum, I learned that up at White Bridge the road gang had worked on through the night. By midnight the stream had became a flood-driven torrent, tumbling boulders and timber before it. But at the bottom of caissons driven into rock for new footings, the workers saw no reason to stop.

Arthur's Pass village, New Zealand's only true alpine village, lies at the centre of the national park. I was first attracted here by the untainted pioneer beauty of the cabins sprinkled through the beech-clad valley that runs down from the highway. A walk along the shingle paths of the village at night—as the cold sets in and the windows start to glow like storm lanterns and chimney smoke curls through the trees—is like entering the pages of a Hans Christian Andersen fairy tale.

The original residents had the foresight to plant beech everywhere, but also decreed there would be no fences. The result is a flowing form to the village, uninterrupted by the usual sense of petty suburban allotment that destroys so much New Zealand streetscape.

Peek into the cabin interiors and you will spy brass beds, ancient flyfishing rods, glorious wood-grained skis and stone fireplaces. Wirelesses are set permanently to the National Programme. Relief maps are framed on the wall.

Among these cabins is the most beautiful church in the world—not that you'd pick it from the outside. But draw open the doors and high on the opposite end wall, framed by clear glass, is a crystal waterfall that

Right Arthur's Pass and Goldney Ridge.

launches from the mountainside, leaping and tumbling and endless. Somehow the framed waterfall is perfectly positioned, there above this quiet place of worship, to settle all argument that seeks to reduce by science or superstition the unknowable random power of life. I shifted my eyes and saw that the lectern and communion rail were a gift from a family whose son, Samuel Russell, died in the waterfall's catchment. I felt in my bones the comfort of this place of refuge and certainty among the ice and rock of the mountains.

Just the night before I had been high in those mountains of the national park with my thirteen-year-old daughter. I was slightly anxious. We'd climbed for some hours through an endless alpine garden, through grandfather beech, bearded with lichen. In the gathering dusk our hut was still a good distance ahead, somewhere near the snowline. Zinzi—city-slacker to the core—was new to this. She was getting restless, was bored with the effort of the climb, the way the straps of her pack dug into her shoulders. She wanted to change channels—the urban reflex.

I pointed out the position of the sun, a few inches above the western peaks. I gently explained that when it disappeared behind the mountains we would be in real trouble. 'We have to find the hut before dark. We have no choice. There is no choice. There is no mall. No KFC. There is just you and me, this mountain and the sun. Nothing else counts or matters.'

I knew we had plenty of time, but I wanted to see my daughter reach inside, to encounter her own strength. Wanted to see a response beyond the usual litany of LA-speak, beyond 'whatever'. And there, in the freezing mountain air, I could see a meditation at work within her. An adulthood at work.

She shouldered her pack. Found her strength. Now the only sounds were the squelch of boots in bog and our breathing, as she led—becoming someone I had never seen before. A transformation among these massive clean clear mountains. The crystal air. Sharp blue sky.

That night, safe within the corrugated-iron walls of true shelter—a mustering hut from the turn of the nineteenth century, framed with raw smoke-blackened logs and tagged with ancient carved initials—I studied my daughter's face. We'd finished the stew, and in the firelight alone together were sharing a mug of black billy tea.

She had been first to spot the hut, had been welcomed by screeching kea, and then together we gathered wood, prising frozen branches from the snow. She set the candles while I set the fire. Nervous of my skill, I used a plastic drink bottle as a mini-bellows. It was bitterly cold. We needed that fire. And now her eyes sparkled.

There is nothing unusual in these mountains about experiencing that powerful sense of human refuge. Nothing unusual, either, about being caught out up here. Constable Niall Shepherd confirmed the danger. 'There are people still up there, lost forever in the mountains. The thing about Arthur's Pass is that this is one of the few roads in New Zealand that takes people right up against severe alpine conditions. In most of the other alpine regions you have to walk in for some days to reach these sorts of conditions, which presupposes some experience. Here you can slam the car door and five minutes later you're in avalanche country.'

Twice a day the Trans Alpine train passes through this world. Up front in the cab on one journey I talked with Alastair Cumming, 20 years a driver. As we traced the crumbling edges of a river gorge, launching out across one viaduct after another, a squall of sleet hit the windscreen. The wipers flopped feebly at the glass. In a reflex response to the sudden blindness, Cumming hit the horn.

Being alone in the cab doesn't make it any easier for a driver to face down the fear of a derailment. Back in the days when rail was king, there would be a crew of three—three pairs of eyes and the support of other trained men to carry the journey. They have been replaced by a vigilance alarm that beeps at intervals. If the driver fails to silence the alarm, it turns into a klaxon and the brakes switch on automatically.

Right McGrath Creek, alongside Coral Track, one of the approaches to Mt Rolleston.

Arthur's Pass National Park

Out from Arthur's Pass the train disappeared into the Otira tunnel, a time-travel tube that in the space of a few minutes delivered us from von Trapp country to Costa Rica. Here on the West Coast an enormous rainfall has sprouted a jungle, on that day frosted with snow.

True to form, there was heavy rain. The rainforest mountains shouldering in above us were shrouded in bruise-black cloud. High in the gloom, seams of silver shone where freshly spawned waterfalls poured over cliffs. A hundred and fifty years ago, to the English settlers concentrated in coastal Canterbury, the fabled lands of the interior were a place of untold terrors. The idea of any connection through the mountains was seen as madness. Coasters, for their part, complained that any road linking them with Christchurch would lead to outside control. They were perfectly happy for their contact with the world to be via the ship to Melbourne, Australia.

But on March 15, 1866 the first coach, with one passenger, made the journey, establishing a tenuous link. On average, in that early period the road was utterly destroyed every second winter. There had been an earlier mail service, a pony express that required rider and horse to swim rivers no fewer than 27 times on each journey.

Even within the confines of a museum, stagecoaches are awe-inspiring contraptions, but lurching down ledges among waterfall and rock, with up to 17 passengers suspended on leather straps, they must have constituted a true nightmare.

Travellers have told of the squeal of iron rims on rock, the staggering and bracing and sweating of horses before the whip. Coach drivers were competitive and often attempted foolhardy river crossings, relying on the current to carry coach, horse and passengers downstream to landfall. It is recorded that after enduring the gorge, many passengers refused the return journey, preferring to travel by sea to Christchurch via Melbourne.

But the pass became a fixture, and, just like the road-builders before them, the current team has brought life to the village. There have been enough children to keep the school open—though sometimes only just. A sun-flooded open structure of alpine stone with windows looking out to mountains, the school, for a child, must be a place of dreams. A villager told me of the teacher who read to them daily from Tolkien and who built a *Lord of the Rings* map in the children's minds of their mountain home. 'Gandalf's lair was up behind the school. We had tracks all over the place.'

On a snowy day in Arthur's Pass I took my daughter up the Rolleston track. She was entranced by the custard-yellow shagpile moss that carpeted the forest floor. Dotted among the moss were tiny plants with bright purple globular fruit that looked to have been planted from a miniature alien spacecraft. We sprawled on our backs on this cushion and looked up at snowflakes drifting through the treetops. For some reason Zinzi had insisted on wearing a fur coat, and like a Dr Zhivago countess seeking exile she climbed without complaint further into the snowfall. Higher up the valley we stopped at the avalanche sign and sheltered in the cleft of a rock. We imagined Maori rock drawings concealed beneath the moss.

The snow eased and we returned to the stream, to the waterfalls gushing champagne into pools whose depths were a cool minted green. We scanned the stream-bed gravel for gold nuggets. Zinzi wanted to build a dam—a different proposition here from the sandy lagoons of home. As she worked, hauling boulders about, she worried about frostbite. She found a stick to lever the larger boulders into final position, and created a diversion channel so her dam would not be overwhelmed.

A city girl in a fur coat, lost in her work. The compulsion of creation, an instinct that surveyor Arthur Dobson—Arthur of the pass—and all those who followed him would have understood. The rich, full sound of the river.

Writing this back in Auckland the images are as strong as ever: My daughter and I in a musterer's hut; the grand icy alpine night settling on the mountains around us; stepping lightly into the morning sun; building a

Left Beech forest and waterfall along the Bealey River.
Above Rushing waters on Otira River, Otira Gorge.
Right A more gentle cascade along the Bridal Veil Walk, a ninety-minute round-trip from Arthur's Pass village.

More than a million hectares in extent, Fiordland is primeval, remote and spectacular—as befits the country's largest national park.

Fiordland National Park
Southern sanctuary Kennedy Warne

Storm clouds have clamped down hard on the Darran Mountains, and in the Hollyford Valley the forest is misty and dark. A confetti of beech leaves drifts from the canopy, splashing the path with red and gold. Tresses of moss, beaded with raindrops, trail from every branch. I am on the track to Lake Marian, one of hundreds of alpine lakes that dot the map of Fiordland National Park like blue tears. Beyond the mountains, which rise in Himalayan profusion in this northern part of the park, lie the Tasman Sea and the fiords—fourteen jagged knife-cuts in the coastline that give the region its name.

With the cowl of my rain jacket pulled over my head, I feel like a monk on his way to vespers in a living cathedral. A tree fuchsia beside the path gently sheds its magenta blossoms. At its foot, where the ground is dry, I pick up paper-thin peelings of orange bark. A South Island robin, elegant in smoky grey, hops onto the path on matchstick legs and cocks her head in my direction. Fern fronds lift their uncurled tips like little fists. Maori steam and eat these young *koru*. I pop one into my mouth. It has a peppery tang, not unpleasant.

The track snakes around trees, dips beneath toppled trunks, crosses streams, then crosses back again. Sometimes the trail is the streambed itself, or a set of steps chainsawn into a log, or a couple of stout tree ferns tossed across a mire. Most of Fiordland's 500 km (312 miles) of walking paths are like this one—soft on the sole and close to nature. Often they are just a more trodden version of the forest floor, twisting threads in a rich carpet of yellows, browns, and greens. Especially greens. From mosses that form verdant cushions on rock and tree root to streams that glow liquid emerald in the sun, this place is an extravagance of greenness. In 1990, when Fiordland and two neighbouring national parks were listed as a United Nations World Heritage Site, the area's most precious natural resource—jade—was chosen for its name: Te Wahi Pounamu, 'the place of greenstone'.

In Maori mythology the South Island is the canoe from which a mighty ancestor, Maui, hauled the fish-shaped North Island out of the sea. Scientists, too, use a nautical image to describe the evolutionary history of these islands: an 80-million-year geological voyage through the Pacific Ocean.

Fiordland's rocks and landforms tell the story of that journey, and because this region straddles one of Earth's most active tectonic boundaries, where two crustal plates scrummage against each other, the outcome is dramatic. Fiordland has been twisted, buckled, folded, and tilted. It has been crushed beneath the ocean sediments for millions of years, then thrust above the waves for wind, sun, and ice to carve and erode. It has been splintered by faults, rocked by earthquakes and frozen by an ice cap a mile thick.

The earthworks continue. Today the razorbacks that mark the eastern edge of the plate boundary are being pushed upward a centimetre a year. Were it not for erosion, some of these peaks would be 20 km (12 miles) high. And although most of the glaciers melted at the end of the last Ice Age, a few continue to scour the high places.

Right Mitre Peak, Milford Sound at high tide.

Lake Marian herself is an ice child. I pick my way along a shore of boulders plucked from the encircling mountains and tumbled in slow motion by the glacier that hollowed out the lake bed. Across the water, clouds swirl about like gauzy curtains, hiding, then revealing, the wooded slopes. Fiordland seems in every sense a work in progress, Earth's unfinished symphony.

Out of a geological maelstrom, strange and wonderful plants and animals have emerged, including several hundred species found only within the park boundaries. Other species, which once enjoyed a wide distribution across New Zealand, now cling to survival only in Fiordland. The most celebrated example is the takahe, the world's largest swamp hen, a turkey-sized bird that was considered extinct for 50 years until deer hunters found a pair in the Murchison Mountains in 1948. It turned out that several hundred takahe were holed up virtually within sight of the town of Te Anau, Fiordland's gateway.

From the air it is not hard to see how a species could be overlooked in such a hinterland. The helicopter taking me up the Snag Burn valley into takahe country feels no bigger than a gnat, which a sudden gust could swat against the granite walls. The ramparts disappear into cloud, and freshly charged waterfalls tumble down their faces.

In this lost world I find the Snag's resident pair of takahe feeding quietly by a stream. They are beautiful birds—an oil painter's dream—with plumage ranging from indigo through iridescent green to licks of chocolate brown, cranberry-red legs and a snow-white rump. I watch as they yank clumps of snowgrass out of the ground with their great red beaks, then pulverise the juicy stalks to extract some meagre goodness.

It's a hard life for a grazing bird in these mountains, where snow blankets the grassy flats in winter. Despite a captive breeding programme, the population is barely holding its own at around 100 birds. The problem for takahe—and for countless other native species—is predatory mammals, all introduced either by accident or through misguided intention by settlers. Before people arrived, reptiles and birds were the dominant vertebrates. Mammals overturned that old order. Against sharp-toothed rodents, stoats, weasels and feral cats, New Zealand's flightless birds—along with giant insects and snails, ground-nesting lizards and frogs—are helpless.

As I watch the takahe, the male starts chasing the female round and round a sapling, stumpy wings lifted and white tail fluffed. The courtship display is short-lived. He gives a soft *harrumph*, then gets back to feeding. Both birds occasionally stop to scratch sandflies out of their eyes with their toes, their metal identification bracelets jangling.

Every paradise has its price, and in Fiordland it takes the form of a blood tribute extracted by hordes of these biting insects. Maori legend has it that Hinenui-te-po, goddess of the underworld, created the sandfly to keep humans from becoming idle in the face of Fiordland's stunning beauty. She succeeded. When visiting Fiordland, the rule is: Keep moving and carry a big can of insect repellent.

Fiordland's curving coastline and narrow fiords, with their multiple arms and countless islands and coves, beckon the explorer to leave the forests and put to sea. At Milford Sound, the northernmost fiord, I hitch a ride on the Department of Conservation's boat, *Renown*. It's going south to Chalky Island, where conservation staff are eradicating stoats to create a new wildlife reserve.

At Milford's commercial wharf—well hidden from the smart tourist jetties—fishing-boat crews are sorting gear and complaining about the lobster price. A forklift scoots about, delivering boxes of bait. Beyond a scraggle of sheds stands Mitre Peak, Milford's craggy eminence. Sea kayakers slice the sea's mirror blackness with their shiny craft.

When he saw Milford Sound for the first time, Donald Sutherland—sealer, soldier and gold prospector— declared, 'If ever I come to anchor it will be here.' He kept his word and in 1878 built three thatched huts, which he called the City of Milford. A dozen years later, when a walking track was put through between

Above Small alpine tarn on Key Summit with the Darran Mountains as a backdrop, Routeburn Track.

Te Anau and Milford, Sutherland opened a boarding house for 'asphalters'—city folk who came to partake of Fiordland's grandeur.

Still they come—half a million a year—some crossing the mountains on the famous Milford Track, most in tour buses on Fiordland's only paved road. The day-trippers take a cruise and maybe a scenic flight, then rejoin the cavalcade back to Te Anau.

There is a stiff breeze today in the outer fiord, flaying the waterfalls that plunge down the sea cliffs, but once we clear the entrance, it dies away to barely a puff, and we steam south on an oily swell. Albatrosses soar in endless lazy arcs. Headlands slide past, each with the same rumpled forest cover, as if an old green blanket had been thrown across them. The glacier-carved fiords, like crooked fingers pointing inland, hide their entrances in sea haze. I tick them off as we pass: Sutherland Sound, Bligh Sound, then George, Caswell, Charles, Thompson, and Doubtful sounds.

In Maori mythology the fiords are the workmanship not of brawny rivers of ice but of an adze-wielding superman, Tu-te-raki-whanoa, who sliced indentations into the wave-battered coastline to make it habitable. But habitation has always been thin. Maori made seasonal visits to hunt and fish and to collect tangiwai, a type of greenstone, from Milford Sound; and from time to time vanquished tribal groups found sanctuary here, living the lonely life of refugees amid the seals and penguins.

James Cook was the first European to set foot in Fiordland. After an epic crossing of the Southern Ocean in 1773 in search of a great southern continent, Cook's ship *Resolution* spent five weeks moored in tiny Pickersgill Harbour, near the southern entrance of Dusky Sound. Outwardly little has changed since Cook's day. Here is the 'murmuring rivulet' that supplied his fresh water; there the stands of rimu (Cook called them spruce) from which he brewed beer to stave off scurvy among his crew. A tree limb leans out over the water in almost the exact position as the one he used for a gangplank. On Astronomers Point the stumps of trees felled so that an observatory could be set up are still plainly visible, gently crumbling beneath a cloak of kidney fern.

In sheltered coves around the seaward islands, fur seal pups drowse on little grass-topped islets. Slaughtered for their pelts in the years following Cook's voyage, Fiordland's fur seals dwindled to the point of extinction but are now on the increase—one of the few native species to post a positive result on Fiordland's balance sheet. The pups raise their heads and fix their lachrymose eyes on us as *Renown* passes.

We press southward to Preservation Inlet, the last fiord. Here, on Fiordland's south-western tip, stands Puysegur Point lighthouse. For a century—apart from a blackout during World War II and the time a lunatic tried to burn down the tower—its beam protected ships navigating this stormy coast. Puysegur is a wild place. The prevailing winds, sweeping up from the Antarctic, smack into this knuckle of land first, before dumping their moisture on the high peaks farther north. Sometimes, during a gale, young relieving keepers would stagger to the edge of the cliff, hold their oilskin coats out wide and lean forward until they lost their balance, trusting the wind to catch them and push them back. The keepers reckoned that if a man had the nerve for this sport, he would never lack for courage for the rest of his life.

Nobody lives here now. The lighthouse was decommissioned in 1980, and two automated beacons took its place. The day I climb the track from the beach to the abandoned station is uncannily calm. For once the Roaring Forties have held their breath. I stand at the edge of the cliff in a cloud of sandflies and try to imagine those daredevil birdmen leaning into the void.

Below me, 30 m (100 ft) straight down, bull kelp writhes in the surf. Lobster boats work the offshore reefs. To the north, land and sea meet in a confusion of islands and zig-zag waterways. Inland, the same ragged tumult of mountains that James Cook described as 'so crowded together as to leave room for no valleys of extent' spreads out to the horizon. The landscapes of Fiordland do not soothe. Their chiselled features preserve the memory of violent upheaval—tattoos on the hull of Maui's great canoe.

Left Bowen Falls, Milford Sound.

Left View towards the Darran
Mountains from Key Summit,
Routeburn Track.
Right Routeburn Track enters moss-
and lichen-coated beech forest at
Lake Mackenzie.
Below Cascade along the
Routeburn Track near Sunny Creek.

Above Fog highlights the foothills
of the Livingston Mountains as
seen from Eglinton Flat.
Right Lyttles Flat view with peak of
the Darran Mountains.

Above Doubtful Sound. First Arm
and Mount Forbes.
Right A waterfall plunges down
the steep sides of Doubtful Sound.

Above Headwaters of the Clinton
River, seen from the Milford Track
at Mackinnon Pass.
Left Boulder and cascade in the
upper Clinton Canyon, Milford
Track.

New Zealand's answer to Mt Fuji, Taranaki (Mt Egmont) stands in majestic isolation as the centrepiece of the country's second-oldest national park. The beauty of its snow-topped cone belies the fact that it could erupt at any time.

Egmont National Park

Born of fire Carl Walrond

On a map of Egmont National Park it looks as if someone has dug a compass into the volcano's summit and inscribed a circle around it. A circle with a radius of 9.6 km (6 miles), to be exact. Outside is farmland, inside is rainforest. Crossing the boundary is like driving into a wall of vegetation. This abrupt demarcation was created in 1881 when Mt Egmont/Taranaki was set aside as a reserve. The original intent was to protect the mountain's flanks 'for the growth and preservation of timber'. With forest in lowland areas reduced to ashes and stumps, it soon dawned on settlers that burning steeper slopes in a high-rainfall area would cause problems. In 1900, the reserve became a national park, the country's second.

As my car gains altitude I am glad of the grader that came through the day before, clearing snow from the road. At the North Egmont car park people sun themselves in the weak July rays. A Department of Conservation officer scrapes ice from beneath the tyres of stuck cars with a shovel. Snowmelt has run onto the asphalt, but by late afternoon at 900 m (2950 ft) it has frozen again.

I shoulder my pack and set off on the low-altitude Round-the-Mountain Track. Being midwinter, the shorter high-level track is snowbound and not an option. So I enter what trampers call 'the green cage'—the forest world.

The dominant trees are kamahi, their boughs draped with mosses, liverworts and filmy ferns. Rain has drawn out the forest colours, and horopito shrubs glow in the glades and gullies. The absence of beech—a signature tree at this altitude—is thought to be due to its inability to recolonise following a volcanic eruption. Taranaki has erupted eight times in the past 500 years, and will certainly do so again.

I pause beside some mountain cedars. A thick branch juts out from one of the trees less than 30 cm (12 in) from the ground. This tree lacks the cedar's usual root buttresses, too. How could this be? Then I remember reading that in some old trees bits of pumice have been found in the boughs. Many trees survive small eruptions, even though partly buried. This is one—a tree without a trunk.

The dissected terrain reminds me of the North West Circuit on Stewart Island. That track follows the coast, crossing the grain of the land. It is the same story here—I drop into one gully only to clamber up the other side and down into the next one.

The mountain has a presence that seems energised in the heavy rain. Most creeks are a strong tea colour, but one is an angry grey—the result of erosion. Another smells of rust, and a coating of ochre has formed on the ferns and grasses at its edge. I smear the stuff on my hands—it feels smooth and cool. Local Maori collected ochre—kokowai—of various hues from such sources, mixing it with shark oil to colour their carvings. The creek reminds me of flooded African rivers, but this isn't a clay-based stain, rather colour that has leached from the broken earth—portent of the fire within.

Right Mt Taranaki volcano emerges above ferns on Lake Mangamahoe.

I stop for some soup at Stratford Mountain House, which accommodates trampers who enjoy their creature comforts. This eastern side of the mountain is the most developed. Three sealed roads lead right into the heart of the national park—at North Egmont, Dawson Falls and here at Stratford Mountain House. Today's building is a far cry from the original, with its iron roof and canvas sides. Built on the Stratford Plateau in February 1899, it was shifted to this lower altitude in 1908 to escape 'inhuman weather conditions'.

Flicking through scrapbooks in the lounge, I come upon a photograph of a group of Maori at nearby Victoria Falls. Their bright orange habits grab my eye. These devotees are Morehu, members of the Ratana Church, who make pilgrimages to the waterfall. The founder of their movement used to go there to meditate and pray, and it has become a sacred site for his followers.

Reclining in the comfort of the café, I have no desire to change back into my cold, wet tramping clothes, but I know the old bush motto: never leave your dry gear on. So, pasting on sodden polypropylene, I prepare to re-enter the dank forest. In fading light I arrive at Lake Dive Hut, so named because of a small lake that has ponded behind one of two curiously shaped humps called the Beehives. These protuberances, termed cumulodomes, formed as lava oozed from the shattered mountain during its formation 130,000 years ago.

The following morning I steadily lose altitude before branching onto Taungatara Track, a trail well endowed with viscous bogs, ankle-twisting roots and other hazards. The streams are up, and I negotiate them with utmost care—more people die in the mountains from drowning than from avalanches or any other cause. Late in the day, as I scramble down the ridge opposite Waiaua Gorge Hut, the river's jet-engine roar makes me think I'll be spending a night in the bush. At the water's edge it's not an easy call. I survey upstream and downstream. At one potential crossing point there is a large midstream boulder with an eddy swirling behind it. I cut a horopito wading stick to test the depth and current. The water comes up to my waist, and as I lunge for the boulder it reaches chest height, but I'm safe here in the slack water. I catch my breath, then complete the crossing and climb a ladder to the cliff top, relieved at my safe arrival.

In the hut book I find an entry by Gareth and Peter from December 1999. 'Spent night in a hollowed-out tree in Waiaua Gorge—very cold and wet.' Cold and wet, but alive. People have died because of visions of dry huts. In 1996, a tramper in the park drowned trying to cross swollen Peters Stream. She knew Holly Hut was on the far bank, and that knowledge killed her. When the warmth of a hut stove is but five minutes away, it's a strong will that can sit shivering in the bush.

Another entry in the hut book refers to Egmont/Taranaki as 'the Mount Fuji of New Zealand'. While Fuji holds a hallowed place in the collective consciousness of the Japanese, its commercialisation and tourist hordes means it is hardly comparable to this pristine peak. About the only things the two peaks have in common are their shape, both being steep, conical volcanoes known as stratovolcanoes, and the way they suffuse the psyche of people—in Japan at the national level, in New Zealand the provincial.

On day three I have barely left the hut when I come across a sign: 'Warning! Mudslide potential. Do not enter riverbed in high rainfall.' Convincing myself the passing shower doesn't qualify as high rainfall I thread my way through piles of rubble and shattered trees. This damage was caused by a major collapse of Taranaki's West Ridge in 1998, which sent a lahar of ice, water, mud and boulders avalanching down Oaonui Stream. Estimated to have dislodged a million cubic metres (35.3 million cubic feet) of material, the landslide was just a small demonstration of the mountain's instability—a 'normal event' in the language of avalanche expert Mauri McSaveney of the Institute of Geological and Nuclear Sciences.

Taranaki is a mélange of unconsolidated rock and ash interspersed with lava flows. Friction holds it together, while gravity and water threaten to tear it apart, and occasionally succeed in doing so. McSaveney has a rather laconic view of the mountain's stability: 'If you could build a mountain that was perfectly designed to collapse, Taranaki would be it.'

Above Mount Taranaki from along Veronica Loop Track.

Egmont National Park

I climb above the bush to Kahui Hut, where entries in the hut book refer to the nearby sacred site of Te Maru Pa, an ancient refuge of Taranaki iwi (tribes) in times of war. One note speaks movingly of a mountain Maori consider to have been unjustly confiscated. 'Stand, our respected elder, repository of our ancestors' knowledge. Take away the heart of the flax bush and where will the bellbird sing?'

In the aftermath of the wars of the 1860s, Mt Taranaki was included in the half a million hectares (1.2 million acres) of land confiscated by the Crown. Maori have pressed for the mountain's return ever since. In 1978, they fleetingly succeeded. In a two-minute meeting at Owae marae, in Waitara, government representatives, under the terms of the newly passed Mount Egmont Vesting Act, vested the mountain in the Taranaki Maori Trust Board, which promptly returned it to the government as a gift to the nation. It seems doubtful that all Taranaki iwi would have agreed to this piece of political sleight of hand, because at the time Maori were lobbying for the return of the mountain and $10 million in reparation. Accordingly, some Maori began referring to Taranaki as the 'magic mountain'—now you have it, now you don't. All eight Taranaki iwi have traditional links with the mountain and have lodged claims with the Crown for its return, along with much additional land. Processing the claim is likely to take many years; meantime, Maori lament the continued loss of mana they experience while 'the heart of the flax bush' remains in government ownership.

As I push on towards Holly Hut, a window in the cloud reveals heavy snowfalls on the upper slopes. The *kek-kek* sound of two falcons floats down to me. The birds are sharp against the cloud as they chase each other over the ridge. Peculiar landforms here, named Big and Little Pyramid, mimic the mountain—cones in miniature. Rain comes again, heavily. This night I can't sleep. Standing out on the hut veranda I wait and watch. Every few minutes a blue-white flash silhouettes the ridgeline as an electrical storm plays itself out far to the south—so distant I don't even hear the thunder. Cold drives me back inside.

On my last day the track climbs up towards Humphries Castle, a fang of rock that jabs into the sky. The leaves of five-finger flash their white undersides as a sou'wester blasts the exposed ridge. There is no need to guess the direction of the prevailing wind. The tips of kaikawaka, the mountain cedar, which thrust above the main canopy, display a distinctive 'flag form,' the foliage appearing to stream out on the tree's downwind side. The kaikawaka are assailed not just by salt-laden winds off the Tasman Sea, but also, in winter, by katabatic winds from the snowfields above.

As I walk on, cloud lifts to reveal Ahukawakawa Swamp, then closes in again, a prelude to hail and sleet squalls. The harsh conditions are hardly surprising. Rising out of a flat plain, the mountain catches weather from every quarter and is one of the most exposed alpine areas in the country. Early European settlers referred to it as 'the rainmaker', and Ngati Ruanui, living on its eastern flanks, call it Pukehaupapa—ice mountain.

Sleet turns to snow as I reach a bend near Boomerang Slip. The track climbs to 1300 m (4263 ft). Further round the steep faces I spot a recent slip below cliffs of columnar basalt. It spills down the slope from a fresh scar on the mountainside, obliterating the track and scouring out the creek bed far below. When I reach the slip I don't linger among the pulverised leatherwood trunks—they resemble human bones. I find it unnerving to be walking on an immense rubble pile only thinly clad with vegetation.

There is nothing secure about this mountain. Perhaps that is part of its mana, its allure. Its postcard symmetry conceals a threat. It is a creator and a destroyer. The rich, butterfat-yielding soils surrounding it were born in a purgatory of brimstone and lahars. One thing is certain: Taranaki cannot be ignored. In most alpine areas a peak can be lost in the landscape, one mountain among many. Not here. Taranaki is so immediate it challenges all who visit it, or who live in its shadow. It defines the landscape—a landscape it has created through repeated eruption and collapse of its unstable cone. It is a national treasure, an island of native biodiversity in a sea of farmland, a noble ancestor, a commercial icon, a provincial symbol and, perhaps most critically, a living volcano.

Left Mount Taranaki with rhododendrons and Lake Mangamahoe.

Above Veronica Loop Track winds
through the subalpine goblin forest
of North Egmont.
Above right Small cascade and
boulders, North Egmont.
Right Fern façade in cloud forest,
Dawson Falls area.

Above Mount Taranaki looking from
northeast.
Right Mount Taranaki rising above
the forest edge, Rahiri.

As if to balance the vast expanse of Fiordland National Park in the south-west of the South Island, Kahurangi National Park—the country's second largest—protects a diverse hinterland in the north-west. Renown for its mountains, rivers and alpine plateaus, Kahurangi also boasts an intimidating coastline.

Kahurangi National Park
The impassable coast Gerald Hindmarsh

To me it will always be the 'impassable coast'—a section of primeval coastline north of the Heaphy River on the western edge of Kahurangi National Park. It has always attracted me: an area so harsh and inaccessible that it has remained virtually untouched by humans. A wild place that deprives of comfort, replenishes the soul and reminds us what this country once looked like.

In 1846 Charles Heaphy and Thomas Brunner explored the area—a marathon journey that took them five months and was described by a contemporary as 'the most arduous expedition which has yet been undertaken in New Zealand'. A century and a half later I began to imagine a trip that followed in the footsteps—and handholds—of those intrepid explorers.

As ambition ripened into obsession, I persuaded three fellow Golden Bay residents to join me. We would follow the coast from the Anatori River southwards to the Heaphy River, where we would connect with the Heaphy Track—Kahurangi's most famous hiking track—and return home. Although our intended route was only part of Heaphy and Brunner's trek, it represented the most difficult and unmodified coastal section.

Setting a date two months ahead, to coincide with especially low spring tides, gave us time to 'train' together, as we jokingly called it. In fact, our training consisted of short, sharp day walks to various peaks in Kahurangi National Park, right on our back doorstep.

The tide was high but ebbing as we set out on the journey proper, fording the Anatori River, making our way over giant blue siltstone rocks that had fallen from the cliffs and scrambling around bluffs between waves. This section of coast isn't part of the national park, and much of it is farmed. Where fences peter out under windblown dunes the cattle come down to wander the beach. Near Kahurangi Point one remarkable dune intrudes into the forest and acts as a giant marker for trampers. Constantly replenished by sand blown up from the coast, it surrounds and envelops fully grown rata trees.

From the outset, Brunner and Heaphy were hampered by bad weather. After a throat-deep crossing of Big River they took refuge in a cave. 'Wet through during the whole of the day,' wrote Heaphy in his journal. The next day: 'Rain and thick weather,' followed by a day of 'strong S.W. gales and rain'. Finally making camp at the Kahurangi River, Heaphy and Brunner discussed the warning given to them by Eneho, an old Maori at Westhaven Inlet only days before, that 'we should never reach Kawatiri, as any white man could not fail to be expended on the coast which lay near Rocky Point and the old rascal and his companions grinned when he mentioned Tauparikaka Cliff as the utmost possible limit of our journeying'.

My companions and I received warnings of our own from cattle musterers with whom we shared the relative comfort of the old lighthouse keeper's house at Kahurangi. 'We had to rescue the last bloke that tried and fell in,' said one. 'You'll be back this way Sunday. They all turn back,' intoned another. It had become a

Right Oparara River, Karamea.

matter of considerable pride that we succeed, although it would be a safe bet to say that all before us at this point had probably felt the same way. After one recent attempt, recorded in the hut book, a tramper had stated simply: 'Karamea or Bust, and I Bust.'

Next morning, after a hearty bacon-and-eggs breakfast washed down with left-over musterers' stew, we shouldered heavy packs and set off overland for the Kahurangi River, barely making headway as we strained forward into gale-force winds. I thought again of Heaphy: 'Our loads consisted of 35 lb [16 kg] of flour each, with tea, sugar, pearl barley, powder, shot, instruments, books, boots, two blankets, amounting to 80 lb [36 kg] each … being exceedingly fatiguing.' As a mark of respect, I resolved not to complain of pack weight again.

Squalls drove in as we forded the Kahurangi River and boulder-hopped for only a few hundred metres before encountering a sheer bluff. It would be no exaggeration to say that in some places it took 10 minutes to make 10 metres of progress, sweating and swearing up that almost vertical slope. Although the predominantly kiekie scrub afforded good holding, it had obviously adapted well to the extreme coastal climate, forming an almost impenetrable interwoven barrier. We alternated between walking over it, crashing through it and crawling under it.

At the top we compared wounds and made reasonable progress through the rata and manuka before finding a steep slip to descend, only to realise at the bottom what a terrible mistake we had made. We were now sandwiched between the bluff we had just bypassed and another even worse one, with the wind making even sitting difficult. The waves struck the cliffs below us with awesome power. Their relentlessness confuses your equilibrium; sometimes you think you are clinging to a swaying cliff over a motionless sea. Add fierce wind, squally rain and the odd giant wave sending up spray that leaves you saturated and you have one of Nature's headiest cocktails.

Sidling around the cliffs at water level was clearly out of the question. So, despite having vowed only minutes before not to subject ourselves to anymore 'kiekie bashing', we retraced our steps back up the slip to the ridge, before finding a waterfall by which to descend to the coast once more.

The knowledge that we were walking into a natural storehouse gave us the confidence to forage for food en route. We took tea for the billy, but left behind the usual essentials in exchange for an old screwdriver with which to prize paua—the New Zealand abalone—off the rocks, knives and an onion sack to gather it all in. One of our party, with a background in botany, would suggest what berries, plants or fungi might be edible, what seaweed would go well with the paua, or even what green wood could be relied on to burn when wet.

As the journey progressed, we became expert in analysing wave patterns: watching for that extra-large recedence that would allow a headlong dash across boulders before the next wave surged in and covered the whole area in a sweeping breaker. Although emergency procedures had been discussed, it became quietly obvious that there would be little hope of rescue or survival if one of us were swept out by a rogue wave.

We made good progress on the low tide rounding Otukoroiti Point to make camp at Christabel Creek, having covered a bare 4 km (2.5 miles) in just under eight hours. Unable to find any sheltered campsites, we were forced to construct a driftwood wall to stop our tent being blown away. We dined on paua, kina (sea urchins) and sea lettuce as the red sun sank into the ocean.

Heaphy reported eating paua—he called it 'mutton fish'—during his expedition. Although 'resembling India rubber in toughness and colour,' he noted that it 'is very excellent and substantial food for explorers'. When eating sea anemones, however, Heaphy recommended that 'the eyes should be kept tightly shut.'

New Zealand fur seals became numerous as we traversed southward. There were five in the creek near our camp, staring out from under flax bushes before charging past us to the safety of the sea. We would often smell seals before we saw them. Sometimes the stench was overpowering. There are two smells that I shall associate with this coast: the salt-laden smell that accompanies the incessant wind and the fetid smell of seals.

Right Buller River.

Kahurangi National Park

At Seal Bay we came to the first real seal colony. There were newborn pups everywhere, and the bulls were challenging each other for territory. After coming ashore and giving birth to a single pup, the female will mate again some ten days later. Unintentionally, we had chosen this rather intimate time for our intrusion, and had to be continually on our guard against hyperactive males and overprotective females. We observed some ferocious fights—several bulls we came across had suffered terrible wounds and were barely able to move.

Beyond Seal Bay we came to a particularly obtuse bluff. It rose vertically, but we had no alternative other than to strike upwards as best we could, and hope to cross into the mouth of the Moutere River. The few metres of loose, crumbly gravel, the transition zone between bare rock and scrub-line, was often the most tortuous; no foothold or handhold could be trusted.

It was here that I experienced my most terrifying moments, inching upwards in toeholds I had cut with my bowie knife, unable to even call to my companions for help because the words wouldn't come out. To finally grab the lowest flax and pull myself up through the steep kiekie was sweet relief indeed.

A wonderful view of the Moutere River, the first substantial watercourse since Kahurangi, provided an excuse to rest on the small saddle. I felt physically drained, every exposed part of my skin was covered in kiekie cuts—deep incisions that seemed to get more painful by the hour—and I had become separated from the others. I charged downwards, falling and stumbling through the kiekie before finding myself on the edge of a precipice with one of my friends below, shouting instructions on the best descent.

In fading light we chose a campsite just before Rocks Point under a beautiful nikau palm grove, which provided good shelter from the continual wind and rain. Keen to relax, we set up camp within half an hour, finding dry wood, lighting a roaring fire, shucking and frying paua, pitching the tent and getting the sleeping bags ready for the wonderful moment when we could lie down out of the weather and unwind.

Next morning we walked straight into a biting sou'wester and intermittent rain, and had to lean forward and clutch rocks to pull ourselves around Rocks Point. There before us was the almost luxurious sand stretch of Big Bay, with its majestic hills covered in nikau, rata, flax and kiekie, and creeks bubbling through gaps in the greenery and down to the sea.

Rounding one point, we encountered a strange phenomenon: foam driven by the wind and heaped up into drifts that were blown about like snow in a storm. We jumped from rock to rock, probing with sticks among the crashing waves and foam, up to our waists in places.

The final 10-km (6-mile) section to Heaphy Bluff is a palm-strewn golden-sand beach, divided into three sections by Kotaipapa and Whakapoai Points. The granite here is more of a grey colour, with occasional pieces of quartz, conglomerate and other rock types intervening. But this geology changes abruptly at the sheer 200-m (655-ft) limestone cliffs that form Heaphy Bluff—another obstacle that must be scaled, not skirted.

Instead of returning to the coast, we chose this point to cross over into the Heaphy River valley and from there connect with the Heaphy Track, the most famous of Kahurangi National Park's network of tracks.

Darkness was falling, with rain imminent, as we followed a creek down through tangled supplejack, finally breaking out on to the river bank. In front of us was a flood-swollen torrent that defied several attempts to cross. Fighting disappointment and reluctantly letting go our hopes of sleeping in Lewis Hut that night, we climbed back into the dank bush to set up camp in heavy rain. We despaired of crossing the river at all now, and began discussing our options while devouring the mussels collected before we left the coast.

The following morning dawned bright and clear, and, as if in anticlimax, we found a broad, waist-deep ford in the receding water several kilometres upstream. We scrambled through some bush and stood on the Heaphy Track, congratulating each other on our triumph.

We covered the remaining 50 km (31 miles) of the track by the following afternoon, walking into Browns Hut at Bainham with exaggerated handshakes, cheers and humour, then collapsing one by one in exhaustion.

Left Sunset through cabbage trees above Karamea.

Left A quiet pool reflects the lush rainforest rich wih tree ferns, mosses and lichens in the Oparara River Valley.

Below left Along the Oparara River, a pathway winds through mixed beech and podocarp forest.

Below Moria Gate Archway along the Oparara River.

Opposite Walking track through coastal nikau forest north of Karamea.

Above and left Archway Islands at Cape Farewell. Just west of the northernmost tip of Kahurangi National Park, this spectacular coastline is accessed through farmland near Puponga.

For sheer diversity of landscape—from glaciated peaks to secluded river valleys, lofty beech forests to fields of alpine flowers—Mt Aspiring National Park is hard to surpass. Little wonder that it has become a favourite haunt of Otago folk.

Mt Aspiring National Park
A toast to the neighbourhood Derek Grzelewski

I live on the edge of Mt Aspiring National Park, and I could draw its fanged skyline with my eyes closed. Strictly speaking, the pyramid of Black Peak, the unmistakeable canine of the Shark's Tooth and the other serrated mountains that form the view from Wanaka delineate just one edge of the park, but they provide a promise and a warning of what lies within.

The park and its many offerings—its beauty, its wildness, its immensity (the third largest in New Zealand, after Kahurangi and Fiordland)—have fuelled my imagination for more than a decade. After years of semi-nomadic existence, of looking for that special place to put down one's roots, I knew I had found it the moment I arrived in Wanaka, one of the gateway towns to Aspiring.

I once lived in the Swiss Alps, where the people have the concept of *hausberg*, literally a home mountain. The local tradition has it that a person needs a mountain with which he or she has a particularly deep and personal rapport. It needn't be a Matterhorn or Eiger, a simple hill will do; what matters most is the strength of affinity. Your *hausberg* is the hideaway where you play as a child and where later you seek solitude during life's tempests; the place you share with your loved ones and only the closest of friends. It is the landmark that springs to mind when you think of home, the epicentre of your personal heartland.

Although I do not confine myself to a single mountain, Mt Aspiring National Park has come to epitomise just this sort of place for me. It is both a playground and a retreat, a place to go to whenever there is a free moment, the same way a city dweller may head for a favourite park to eat lunch, stroll or walk the dog.

Of course, I'm just one of a countless throng to have come under the spell of the place. As early as 1885, Westland's District Surveyor Gerhard Mueller wrote: 'For grandeur of scenery I do not think there is another spot in New Zealand to equal the Aspiring country.'

Fortunately, the park is so large it can easily accommodate all those enchanted by its beauty, and though its perimeters certainly see a large numbers of visitors, there are also vast spaces in the interior where you can live for a few days or weeks without seeing a soul.

The park straddles the Southern Alps, extending for 140 km (87 miles) between Fiordland and Haast, encompassing 355,543 ha (877,883 acres) of mountains, glaciers and forested river valleys. The nearest towns, and the points of entry into the wilderness, are Te Anau, Glenorchy, Wanaka and Haast, each giving access to a side of Aspiring so uniquely diverse that moving from one to another you could be mistaken in believing you are entering a different park altogether.

The Te Anau side, accessed from the Milford Sound road, is very Fiordland-like; for it is here that the two parks merge, forming the core of the World Heritage area. The Glenorchy aspect, dominated by the forked summit of Mt Earnslaw (literally 'eagle's hill'), is perhaps best described by the names of two nearby hamlets, Paradise and Arcadia, and the fact that many of the *Lord of the Rings* forest scenes were filmed here.

Right Fantail Falls, Haast River. One of the most popular stops on the scenic Haast Highway.

Wanaka lies closest to the glaciated hub of the park, where the flat-topped ice fields of the Bonar, Therma and Volta glaciers terrace the flanks of Mt Aspiring before breaking off over vast cliffs to form glacial cirques. The water from these huge basins is the coldest I've plunged into. It doesn't just take your breath away, it feels like the kiss of Hans Christian Andersen's Snow Queen, instantly freezing the very marrow of your bones.

Then there is Haast, where the Southern Alps slope down to meet the sea, and where the powerful rivers draining the northern side of Mt Aspiring—the Cascade, Arawata and Waiatoto—make their thunderous passage. This section of the park is home to one of the world's rarest creatures, the Haast kiwi—an oddity as elusive as the Himalayan snow leopard, and unlike any kiwi you'd ever encounter. It has white feet, a short, stubby beak and a thick, downy coat the colour of a red deer's fur and as fluffy as that of a husky. It is New Zealand's only alpine kiwi, quite content to spend its winters nesting in rock crevices under half a metre of snow, venturing out on sunny days to probe for invertebrate life—weta, weevils, land snails and the like—made comatose by the cold.

For all its vastness and the unpredictability of its weather, Mt Aspiring National Park is a place to be explored on foot, ideally with a tent and a week's worth of provisions. There is a plethora of tracks and huts—Routeburn, Dart and Cascade Saddle, the Matukituki, Wilkin and Young, to name just the famous ones, but many more whose obscurity guarantees undisturbed solitude and offers the increasingly rare opportunity to lose oneself for a time in true wilderness.

Even on a popular track like the Routeburn, one of the country's designated 'Great Walks,' you have only to wander for a few minutes from the well-groomed trail to find yourself in a landscape little changed since the time of the pioneers. Indeed, imagine a glacier or two and you could be back 10,000 years.

I have walked the 39-km (24-mile) Routeburn Track many times, following its picturesque path through the Humboldt Mountains between Fiordland and Mt Aspiring National Parks. I toasted the New Year with an overspiced punch in a hut warden's quarters, trudged patiently among the Easter crowds and slogged through waist-deep winter snowdrifts. I slept under a kitchen sink in a hut bursting at the seams and, on occasions, I had the entire track to myself. I walked across Lake Harris, frozen so thick you could drive a car over it, and heard the ice groaning in the first of the spring thaw.

One of the epic journeys in the history of New Zealand exploration, the odyssey of gold prospector Alphonse Barrington and his two companions, took place in and around the Mt Aspiring region—though, true to their time and priorities, the party had absolutely no intention of getting lost in the woods and mountains. Hoping to spark a new gold rush, in 1863 the Barrington trio struck up the Routeburn and its North Branch, descended into the Hidden Falls Creek and followed it upstream, then crossed the meadows of Cow Saddle into the headwaters of the Olivine River and down to Lake Alabaster.

They continued on along today's Pyke–Big Bay Track, then followed the Gorge River to its source, over a high saddle and down into the Cascade. Here at last, on fine gravel beaches heaped with quartz boulders and sequined with mica crystals, they found a sufficient amount of gold to justify more lengthy prospecting.

So far, their expedition had been a strenuous but pleasant enough tramp. It was the return trip, however, that degenerated into a survival saga ranking with that of Shackleton's in the Antarctic. During this journey the Barrington trio were to experience the forces that shaped the mountains and rivers of the area in their full grandeur and unbridled fury.

Storm after storm lashed the party. As torrential rain turned into wet snow, freezing as it fell, Barrington became separated from his companions. After nine days alone in his tent, which became buried under a metre of snow, he struck up for Stag Pass, a broad, high-alpine saddle leading into the watershed of Barrier River. He crawled and cursed, collapsing every 20 steps for a brief rest and discarding almost all of his waterlogged belongings—including, some say, his gold—which were now only a burden.

Above **Beech forest in the Humboldt Mountains, Routeburn Track.**

He was finally reunited with his companions, but the worst still lay ahead of them, for they were now on the edge of the Olivine Ice Plateau, a large and isolated pocket of ice from which numerous glaciers ooze out through the palisade of encircling mountains.

Today it would be unthinkable to venture there without ropes, crampons and ice-axes, but they had only their rifles, knives and a tomahawk. They half-walked, half-fell down the glacier, only to have their camp washed away by the flooding Lake Alabaster. 'This is the most miserable day of my existence,' Barrington recounted in his diary. 'The water rose so fast we could not get anything away but our blankets ... Had to walk up and down all night, rain still pouring. If this night does not kill us we shall never die.'

Live on they did, but when the trio finally emerged from the wilderness near Glenorchy they were described as looking like living skeletons covered with skin, so weak they could barely speak.

It is perhaps the measure of our times that the trials and tribulations of those early explorers are to us an enticement and an inspiration, and we seek those very adventures our predecessors tried their best to avoid. One summer I succumbed to the desire to follow in Barrington's footsteps, retracing part of his journey with a friend, Mick Hutchins, a one-time Oxford scholar and at that time a Mt Aspiring National Park ranger.

I envisaged a bucolic journey against a backdrop of *Sound of Music* scenery, with campfire stories thickened with pipe smoke, perhaps with Mick reciting classic pentameters as our marching songs. And I was right. But what I didn't imagine was that barely three days into the trip I'd be clinging for dear life to a handful of vine-like roots overhanging a mossy and near-vertical river bank, mustering all my courage to use them as a pendulum to reach the other side. Or that carrying a backpack with two-weeks' worth of food, camping and climbing equipment was about as pleasant as enduring a fortnight-long crucifixion. Or that Barrington's account, melodramatic as it seemed, was in fact a quiet masterpiece of understatement.

And yet, we were exploring and adventuring in the real meaning of these words, for adventure is what happens when things do not go the way you planned them, and exploring, as Samuel Butler wrote, is always 'delightful to look forward to and back upon, but it is not comfortable at the time, unless it be of such an easy nature as not to deserve the name'.

Our adventures must have been honest and true, for I reflect on them fondly now, and beyond the sweat and blood and blisters I recall the exquisite beauty of kidney ferns dotting fallen tree trunks like flocks of bright green butterflies, and the electric-blue lights of glow-worms sparkling in the undergrowth at night. The rata canopies smouldering with their fiery flowers, the buttercups and edelweiss catching the eye like gemstones. In the forest, the colossal red beeches, straight and smooth like Greek columns, seemed to support the very sky itself, and every creek and river we crossed was so clear you could drink from it.

As the kea flew, we were literally in our own backyards, only a short distance from our respective homes; yet this distance was measured in days, and the time within those days was not measured at all, for doing so would not serve any practical purpose. We were home and we knew it, growing more comfortable with this idea with every passing day. At one time, I watched Mick, who was in front of me and waist-deep in the water, crossing a river. For a moment he was bent double, ducking under an overhanging tree, the heavy pack almost forcing his face into the swift current. Mocking a kiss, he took a sip of water. A toast to Alphonse Barrington, to our journey, to our park.

Left Bridal Veil Falls from Weka Flat, Routeburn Track.

Right Sugar Loaf Stream cascades through a gorge as it approaches Routeburn.
Below right Wild Spaniard blooms among sub-alpine vegetation along the Routeburn Track.
Below Lake Harris and Mount Erebus from the Routeburn Track.

Above The rushing waters of the
Haast River.
Left Moss and lichen coated
cobbles in the Routeburn
streambed.

In the heart of the Southern Alps lies New Zealand's premier alpine area, Mt Cook National Park, a 70,000-ha (172,840-acre) expanse of mountains, glaciers and river valleys that calls to mountaineer and tourist alike.

Mt Cook National Park
A noble viewpoint Derek Grzelewski

Thump-thump — ice-axe, ice-hammer — *thump, thump* — left boot, right boot — *thump, thump* — axe, hammer ... up and up. Two banana-shaped picks and the curved claws of my crampons are my only points of contact with the mountain, the only way of pinning myself to its polished flank. Each stab of steel chips away chunks of ice and sends them hissing down into the white abyss. There, 500 m (1640 ft) below me, the ice wall runs out, gradually losing its steepness and flattening into a glacier cracked with crevasses.

Above me the same wall rears up to form a jagged skyline. I am ascending an invisible stairway to heaven, chiselling the steps as I go. *Thump-thump* ... two more steps, then a brief rest. My two companions also pause. Other than the wheezing of our laboured breaths, the silence is absolute. Almost. I also hear the drum-beat of my pounding heart: *thump-thump, thump-thump*.

We are climbing towards the still distant High Peak of Aoraki/Mount Cook, New Zealand's tallest mountain. High Peak is the apex of Aoraki's three-pronged summit ridge. Shaped by the prevailing nor'westerly winds, the ridge resembles the crest of an ocean wave, frozen just before it breaks.

It was just after midnight—10 hours ago—when the three of us set out from Plateau Hut, a refuge perched above the bowl-shaped Grand Plateau. By starlight—uncommonly brilliant at this altitude—and by the cones of yellow light cast by our head-torches we crossed the fissured hollows of the plateau. Our crampons, squeaking a high-pitched staccato, barely pierced the concrete-hard snow.

Much of the climbing in Mt Cook National Park starts in darkness because at night and early morning the ice and snow are frozen solid, which means you can travel with relative speed and safety. Later in the day the sun, which up here can have the intensity of a welding torch, heats up cornices and the house-sized blocks of ice called séracs, causing them to collapse under their own weight and plummet down as avalanches. The heat also causes snow to acquire the consistency of porridge, sapping all strength from your legs and making every step arduous.

We made our way through the austere labyrinth of the Linda Glacier Icefall, which in the eerie pre-dawn light resembled an ancient metropolis reduced to rubble. Crevasses, mouths agape, sliced the surface like knife wounds. Bridges, caves, arches, tunnels, spires and towers—every imaginable type of ice sculpture was there, garlanded with icicles and frosted with windswept frozen crust.

This approach route to Mt Cook, though technically one of the easiest, is perhaps also the most dangerous, for it crosses and re-crosses gullies, or couloirs, where avalanches roar down with the speed and frequency of express trains. One of the more notorious is called the Gunbarrel.

Once on the flanks of the mountain and above the treacherous ice-fall the climbing was steeper but safer, more a test of skills and a head for heights than the luck of a draw.

The sun, peeping from behind Malte Brun Range, meets us partway up the curtain of ice on which we

Right Aoraki/Mt Cook, New Zealand's highest peak, towers over the glacier-fed Hooker River.

crawl like beetles. Two hours later we rope up to negotiate a craggy barrier known as the Summit Rocks, beyond which a steep slope leads to the top. A sou'westerly howls over the ridge, forcing us to hug the slope. In the lee of the wind-scoured summit cornice we cut a small platform, the only horizontal patch in this vertical world: somewhere to rest, to celebrate, to quench the tormenting thirst.

There is no feeling of conquest, more a sense of relief that we have made it, mixed with anxiety that we are still less than a halfway there. The descent—the less glamorous but more taxing and perilous part of mountaineering—is still ahead of us.

For now, though, we savour the moment: the sea of mountains around us, the frozen silence, hot tea burning crusted lips, the elegant pyramid of nearby Mt Tasman, the undulating summit ridge of Mt Cook, known as New Zealand's 'highest mile.' From here, on a clear day, you can see both coasts and the mightiest of our glaciers, the Tasman Glacier, 29 km (18 miles) long, a ribbon of white winding down to meet the turquoise pool of Lake Pukaki.

The vistas here are so out of scale, so beyond everyday proportions, that it's easy to think you are standing on top of the world. The relative height of Mt Cook, from the base of the glacier moraine to the wind-sculpted summit, approaches 3000 m (9836 ft), and above the flat, desert-like Mackenzie Country the mountain cuts an imposing figure. In April 1860, after seeing it for the first time from a peak in Two Thumb Range, Samuel Butler of *Erewhon* fame wrote: 'No one can mistake it. If a person says he *thinks* he has seen Mount Cook, you may be quite sure that he has not seen it. The moment it comes into sight the exclamation is, 'That is Mount Cook!'—not 'That *must* be Mount Cook!'

Aoraki and its neighbouring mountains are so high they create their own weather, stopping and anchoring the fast-moving clouds, draining them of almost all the moisture they have gathered over the Tasman Sea. It is a climate of extremes, of searing sunshine and icy chill (one of few places where you can get sunburnt and frostbitten at the same time), of days so still you can hear the glacier moving and wind so forceful it can lift you off the ground, pack, ice-axe and all.

Although the tussock highlands of the Mackenzie Basin are parched sepia-brown by almost continuous sunshine, curtains of torrential rain can veil the mountains and fierce winds whip up miniature tornadoes along the flats of the braided Tasman River. Even on clear and seemingly calm days, hogsback clouds, like deformed Napoleonic hats, often cap the summit of Mt Cook, heralding another storm. They are also the reason for the mountain's Maori name, Aoraki, translated as Cloud Piercer or Cloud in the Sky.

The national park to which Mt Cook lends its name and charisma stretches for some 80 km (50 miles) along the Main Divide and contains all nineteen of New Zealand's 3000-m (9836-ft) mountains except for Mt Aspiring. Over 40 per cent of the park is covered by permanent glaciers, and in places the ice is up to 600 m (1967 ft) deep. Together with the adjoining Westland National Park, Mt Cook forms the largest expanse of high-alpine wilderness in the country, and in 1990 the uniqueness of the park was recognised when it was included (along with Fiordland, Mt Aspiring and Westland National Parks) in the Te Wahipounamu—the South West New Zealand World Heritage site.

Despite their frozen appearance, the landscapes of Mt Cook National Park are anything but static. The glaciers are the park's unstoppable, if slow-flowing, rivers (crevasses are the rapids, ice-falls the cataracts). Ever since their birth between two colliding tectonic plates, the mountains have been rising at a rate of about 6 mm (a quarter of an inch) a year. Were it not for weather-induced erosion and the grating of the glaciers, which combine to shear the new growth at almost the same rate, Mt Cook would by now be about 18 km (11 miles) high, and you could see it from the moon.

Then there are the avalanches. Just after midnight on December 14, 1991, some 14 million cubic metres of rock and ice broke off near the top of Mt Cook and rushed down its east face. Funnelling through the

Above An aerial view of Aoraki/Mount Cook, looking towards Lake Pukaki.

Hochstetter Icefall, the gigantic avalanche reached a velocity estimated at 400–600 km/h (250–375 mph), and by the time it crossed the moraine of the Tasman Glacier and eventually petered out, its volume had quadrupled. Had a similar avalanche swept across nearby Mount Cook Village—the only area of habitation in the park—it would have buried the village and its 200-odd permanent residents under a heap of rubble 20 m (66 ft) deep.

There were climbers asleep in Plateau Hut at the time, but the cataclysm missed them, though not by much. They later reported being awestruck by the almost incomprehensible power of nature, devastating yet strangely thrilling and beautiful. Perhaps glimpses of such grandeur, the extremes of calm and fury, are what draw many of us to venture into those mountains, despite their dangers.

I once came to Mt Cook National Park primarily to climb, but now it is more often to ski. In winter, the park is like a piece of the Antarctic and the snow-fall on the upper névés is measured in metres. It fills up crevasses, and conceals rocks and moraines, bringing with it a most profound silence. I once travelled on skis for several days without seeing a soul (except my own). Another time, with several companions, I reached the remote Murchison Hut to find it completely buried under snow, with only the radio aerial visible. On a different occasion I skied to the Barron Saddle Hut, at the top of the Mueller Glacier, and found there three perfectly frozen oranges. A party of climbers departing for Mt Sealy had left them there four months earlier. There were no other visitors in the meantime.

Climbing is sometimes portrayed as a struggle against a lurking menace—'Balancing on a fine line between life and death on sloping holds against the unforgiving force of gravity,' as one climber has put it. Mt Cook itself has been described both as a 'killer mountain' and a 'gigantic graveyard'. And there's some justification in those labels. Since climbing began here over a century ago more than 200 people have died in the mountains of Mt Cook National Park, and climbers have been known to disappear even on the way to a hut toilet. Huts themselves have been blown off their foundations—a challenge to their image as safe havens.

But between and behind headline-making fatalities there are remarkable stories of survival and the human spirit soaring high in this simplified world of do-or-die. For me, time spent in Mt Cook National Park, whether climbing or ski mountaineering, has evoked a roller coaster of emotions and images that have burnt lasting imprints in my memory. The anxiety of departures and the relief of safe returns, fear and elation, utmost misery and unfettered ecstasy, all tightly intertwined, fluctuating with every rope length. Rush of adrenalin, a throat-knotting view and the tang of zinc on sunburnt lips. Squeak of midnight snow underfoot, hiss of rope slithering against the névé and the tale-tell aroma of thermal clothing soaked with sweat and dried by the wind many times over. Fresh taste of water, reassuring warmth of sun and the occasional stream of profanities after the leader's fall into a hidden crevasse.

There is a peculiar quality to these mountains, one which is difficult to communicate without pathos and clichés. Prose and verse invariably fail, paintings and photographs can sometimes capture a glimpse of it, but to me this quality seems more like music—a sensual symphony that leaves much space for individual interpretation and where no two impressions are ever the same.

Mountains represent freedom, a certain loftiness of thought, a release from the entrapments of modern civilisation, a place where, in the words of climber Tom Patey, 'we get a little older in wisdom, a little younger in spirit'. They provide a fresh perspective, a view unhindered by the burden of the small and unimportant. For those seeking this perspective—a way to explore both the inner and outer landscape—the mountains of Mt Cook National Park provide noble viewpoints indeed.

Left Spikes of the native golden Spaniard and glacial boulders with Mount Sefton behind.

Opposite Mount Sefton overlooks trampers enjoying the views from a swing-bridge over the Hooker River.

Above Melt water from the Hooker Glacier, joins that of the Mueller Glacier before flowing into the Hooker River.

Left An early summer highlight for many visitors is the Mount Cook lily, the largest member of the buttercup family.

Right Aoraki/Mount Cook and part of the Main Divide running north above Lake Pukaki.
Right below Aerial view of the east face of Mount Sefton with Mount Brunner to the south.
Below Aoraki/Mount Cook and Mount Hicks (St David's Dome) glow in dawn light, Southern Alps.

Craggy mountains, as much as cold blue lakes, define the geography of Nelson Lakes National Park, which marks the northern end of the Main Divide. Forests of beech, an ancient family of trees, are a feature of the park.

Nelson Lakes National Park
Breakfast and the beech Carl Walrond

Hiking through beech forest is like walking on a carpet of breakfast cereal, where the size and colour of the grains tells you the altitude. Red beech prefers fertile, warm river flats and broad benches. Beside Lake Rotoroa—the larger of the two glacier-carved lakes for which this national park is named—the fallen red beech leaves are the size of big cornflakes.

As my companion and I start to gain altitude, following the Sabine River up into the Spenser Mountains, silver beech appear, with their smaller cornflake leaves. Higher still and mountain beech takes over, their oval leaves like so many rice bubbles scattered over the ground. It takes us five hours to tramp from Sabine Hut, on the shores of Lake Rotoroa (altitude 450 m/1475 ft), to West Sabine Hut (770 m/2459 ft), crunching cereal flakes all the way.

T-shirt-clad in the muggy December weather, we head up-valley towards Blue Lake, stopping to camp at an overhanging rock. We take water from the Sabine, some 20 m (65 ft) away. A bush robin visits, looking unbearably fragile on its too-skinny legs. In the half-light under the rock I make out stacked firewood, and the names and acronyms of tramping clubs scrawled in charcoal on the walls. My failed attempts to light a fire mean an early night. On a bed of rice-bubble leaves we sleep off the exertions of the day.

After the night in our rock den, we set out for the lake again. The track crosses and re-crosses avalanche paths—gullies and fans where the surviving vegetation leans precariously towards the river. The leaves of dead beech and rust-coloured mountain celery pine litter the ground among shattered stumps and branches. In places, bark has been stripped by rocks swept down as part of the churning masses of snow and debris.

The winter of 2004 brought exceptionally heavy snowfalls here. Snow builds up in basins above 1500 m (4918 ft), and when it slips it rushes down gullies and into the valleys. The Department of Conservation recently signposted the sides of each chute with 'Avalanche Path, No Stopping' and 'Avalanche Path Ends,' but avalanches removed so many signs they had to space them further apart. I have to wonder about the department's philosophy and consistency in pointing out this sort of danger. Where are the signs along rivers and bluffs? Few trampers have been killed by avalanches, but many have fallen to their deaths or drowned.

We pass Blue Lake and keep climbing over the ancient landslide that holds back Lake Constance—or almost holds it back; beneath this enormous rubble pile an underground stream trickles into Blue Lake. Climbing scree on the track to Waiau Pass, on the park's southern boundary, we pause on a tussock bench with a view of Lake Constance. Deeper than Blue Lake, it has a gun-metal hue. Grasshoppers spring from tussock to tussock, and butterflies, black-winged to maximise heat absorption in this alpine environment, sit on sun-warmed rocks.

Opposite us broad scree fans slope like grey skirts from the bluffs and ridges of the park's highest point,

Right **Honeydew beech forest fringes Kerr Bay on Lake Rotoiti.**

Mount Franklin (2340 m/7672 ft). On one scree two springs emerge, but disappear back into the stony fan a few hundred metres further down. I make out five specks swimming near the far shore of the lake—to be visible at this range they can only be Canada geese, a pest in this part of the world.

An entry in Blue Lake Hut book reads, 'Pain is inevitable. Suffering is temporary.' To get this deep into the park, some pain and suffering is involved. My feet are blistered. Tramping has a certain masochistic element. To enjoy it, one of the prime requirements is not physical, but mental. When the hill is steep, the pack heavy and camp hours away, an ability to take your mind elsewhere serves well.

As we drop back to our den, re-crossing the avalanche paths, I notice a fresh-faced greywacke block embedded in the track. I follow bent-over saplings down to the river and see that it is a fragment of a larger boulder that had bounded into the river from a scree slope and smashed, spraying shards into the forest.

A little way further along the track are what I took to be windfalls the day before. I now see sharp rocks among these splintered stumps, the bounding boulder's victims. Looking closely, I notice older, moss-covered rocks lying all around like mute witnesses. The new rocks on the block were a few weeks ago adorning a cliff face 1000 m (3279 ft) up.

This park is about right angles. We walk along flat valley floors onto which snow and rocks fall from the adjacent mountains, sweeping everything aside in their path. Sometimes they blast across the river and up the opposite side, where trees lean *uphill*. It is country in which rock and vegetation vie for ascendancy. Lichens change the light-grey active rock-fields to darker hues, so the paths of recent bouncing boulders stand out clearly.

We cook our meal at West Sabine Hut. A father, his teenage son and an army engineer bound for reconstruction work in Afghanistan tell us there are good camp sites about two hours eastward, on the track to Travers Saddle. After dinner we climb through red beech and drop to the upper East Sabine. A kaka whistles noisily. We cross a bridge over a slot canyon. Peering, I struggle to see water in the tight, evil gorge.

Walking past ideal campsites ahead of schedule, we hump up an avalanche chute that doubles as a stream for about 700 vertical metres. There is no level ground, so we are committed to getting to the tops. The track finally levels out on dark, and we weigh down the tent fly with rocks in a tussock basin a few hundred metres below the saddle. There is nothing to drink—the stream in the chute went underground, and the one here is dry. In this rock-strewn land water finds much of its way below ground.

Next morning, after climbing a hundred metres, we look back to see a pond near our campsite, which was hidden by a knob. At a stream we drink. A cool easterly, an unusual wind here, scuds clouds as we reach the 1787-m (5859-ft) saddle. Buttercups and celmisia dot the ground yellow and white.

On the descent, two Canada geese glide past us only metres above the ground, their wings braking as they drop into the Travers. We are left with the image, and the sound of wind soughing past their feathers.

Grant, my companion, was last at Upper Travers Hut some 30 years earlier. That building has gone; the new hut is larger and more palatial (it is double glazed). A small hut warden's quarters adjoins the main building. I am reminded of the popular Kepler and Greenstone Tracks in Fiordland where I worked for two summers as a hut warden. It seems that, in time, the Travers, too, will become a 'Great Walk'—the designation given to the country's most-frequented walking tracks.

The old hut site—just a patch of blackened earth—sits lower on the tussock flats, just past an 'Avalanche Path Ends' sign. It was burnt down, as this is the easiest way to remove old huts. In the 1890s, cattle were run up this valley. Some went wild—three bulls were shot near here around 1900. Of those formidable beasts, one musterer wrote, 'The nearer the buggers got the bigger they got, and the longer the horns.'

After a wash and an early lunch we plod downriver in the rising summer heat towards John Tait Hut, named after a diehard Nelson tramper. Three hours later we drop our packs for a second lunch. Prodding fingers have worn a 'you are here' point on the wall map. A story next to it, written by one of John Tait's

Above Lake Rotoiti from Mount Robert.

daughters, details the original hut's history. Tait's three daughters helped to row the materials up Lake Rotoiti in 1951, and everything was then hauled up the valley. A photograph shows how the awkward chimney cowling was carried—on Tait's head. With his hat sticking out he looks like a New Zealand Ned Kelly. He smoked his pipe in the metal sheath as he sauntered towards where Cupola Creek tumbles to the Travers, and where his vision came to fruition.

A nor'west breeze rains cornflakes from the red beeches. Downstream, I pause to watch a large trout sipping flies from the surface, wishing I had my rod.

When I catch up to Grant at the side track to Hopeless Creek he relates a conversation. Ten minutes after leaving John Tait Hut he told two trampers on the track that the hut was still an hour away. They countered with news that a family was heading up to the small Hopeless Hut. Grant is unsure whether this was their riposte or the awful truth. If a family is holed up there overnight there will be no room for us.

We strain to make out footprints in the muddier parts of the track as we sweat and climb into the side basin. Spots of rain dot stones at a creek. We decide the hut is an hour away at most. A few minutes later I come across it. Swinging the hinges reveals the family. But we are lucky—adjacent to the woodshed there is a low-ceilinged annexe. In the privacy of this oversized dog box I cook. Out the window, the source of a massive shingle fan is hidden in mist. An avalanche in the winter of 2004 came to within 30 m (98 ft) of where I sit, and there were thoughts of putting the hut on skids and moving it further back into the forest. Opened in 1967 by Sir Edmund Hillary, it has stood here long enough that it's a safe bet no avalanche will touch it before its timbers have rotted and its iron roof rusted through.

Morning brings rain and low cloud. A decision on whether to tackle the pass is deferred for some hours by rolling over in the sleeping bag. Later, when the rain fades to drizzle, we climb a steep scree slope with adjacent waterfalls tumbling down bluffs. Just before a small tarn I turn, alerted—a rock clatters to rest in the 100 m (328 ft) between Grant and me. Looking up, I see there are just bluffs and mist. Cairns mark the way through boulder fields that resemble a quarry floor. In remnants of scalloped snow there are patches of red algae, beech leaves, dead moths and other wind-borne fragments. At 1900 m (6230 ft), Sunset Saddle is anything but— though gaps in the cloud appear as we descend, giving snatched views of Hinapouri Tarn and Lake Angelus.

At Lake Angelus Hut we talk with an Australian couple we saw on our first day. They tell of swimming in the Sabine and of Anthony, the talk of the park, a bespectacled English tramper who carried neither sleeping bag nor food yet thought he could get to Lewis Pass—more than twice the distance to Lake Constance—in two days. I last saw him retreating past the rock den early on our first morning. The Australians praise the New Zealand hut system, calling those who don't pay hut fees 'scrounging mongrels'.

On the last leg towards St Arnaud, the picturesque gateway village for Nelson Lakes National Park, we follow the Robert Ridge track above Lake Rotoiti. To our left is Speargrass Valley, where deer trails criss-cross the screes, and on our right are ridges, basins, tarns and rubble fields. Near the end of the ridge are the buildings of a club skifield that grew from humble origins in the 1930s. The skifield went bust in the early 2000s and no one quite knows what to do with it. It is too low for reliable snow. To get to the field skiers had to carry their equipment up the Pinchgut Track—the beech branches above me have been pruned so that carried skis do not snag. The descent is tortuous—a long zigzag to the car park.

Sitting beside steaming boots and socks, I reflect. We went long with light packs, stealing hours after dinner in midsummer, but much remains unseen. I know that names such as Waiau Pass, Faerie Queene, Nardoo (one of the few aboriginal New Zealand place names), even 'unnamed pass'—all the mysterious for having none— will have me poring over topographical maps again. I'm just another addict to the cult of country, of landscape and its possibilities. While pain is inevitable, suffering is temporary, and both are soon forgotten. What remains is an insight into the lie of a shattered land.

Left Red beech forest floor of mosses along the Pinchgut Track, Mount Robert.

Left and Below Old-growth
mountain beech trunks covered in
mosses and lichens.
Below left Design in the moss
along Bellbird Walk, Lake Rotoiti.

Above **Dawn fog on Lake Rotoiti.**
Right **Shoreline grasses along Lake Rotoiti in a storm.**

Created exactly 100 years after the formation of New Zealand's first national park, Paparoa is a place of cliffs, canyons and caves—and the luxuriant rainforest for which the South Island's west coast is renowned.

Paparoa National Park
Ghosts of the forest Derek Grzelewski

Outside my door the sea is breathing heavily. Its exhalations are short and explosive, violent blasts of white water that bulldoze the stony beach and crumble the rocks that guard it. There are brief moments of silence before the sea begins to draw another breath, sucking itself in with a slow asthmatic hiss, raking the gravel as it goes out, gathering itself for another blow.

I am living in a rented bach along the Paparoa coast—my own attempt at Thoreau's cabin in the woods—and this heaving sea is my closest neighbour. The bach, nicknamed the Biscuit Tin, is a simple corrugated iron and plywood affair painted bush-green, with rusty red trimmings, floorboards that slant in every direction and a weathered wooden deck facing the sea. The deck is a museum of the beachcombing existence. There are bits of driftwood that resembled something to someone, stones and shells, a faded buoy, a decaying crayfish pot with a rope stiffened by salt and sun, a blue-and-yellow flipper. My own additions include a stone calendar—a dark grey rock to mark each day's beach walk and a white egg-shaped quartzite for Sundays.

Every day, using leathery flax leaves for handrails, I climb down the steep track leading to the shore. Behind me, a wall of thickly forested mountains—the Paparoa Range—rises sharply, almost parabolically, above the string of cottages that cling to this coastal strip. The fresh broccoli-green of the forest and the steel-grey of the sea with the usually overcast sky—these are the colours of the Paparoas.

The best known features of my neighbourhood are the 'pancake rocks' and blowholes at Punakaiki—a compulsory stop for some 450,000 annual visitors, whose cameras click-clack like cicadas as their owners stroll around the rocky promontory. Every minute or so, particularly when the tide is up and a south-westerly swell is rolling in, there is a guttural rumble as a big wave surges in to fill underground cavities and erupts geyser-like through narrow fissures, spraying the onlookers and sounding as if someone were blowing his nose over a PA system.

The blowholes, a wild coastline bristling with nikau palms, a distant white cloud that on closer examination turns out to be the massif of Mt Cook, perhaps a roadside picnic (inevitably curtailed by voracious sandflies)—for travellers, these may be the lasting impressions of one of the most picturesque drives in the country. They are, however, only postcard snapshots compared to what lies inside Paparoa National Park, a 30,000-ha (74,074-acre) wilderness bounded by the bold summits of the Paparoa Range on one side and the turbulent west coast on the other.

It was local geologist and legendary solo sea kayaker Paul Caffyn who first alerted me to the peculiar lie of the land here. The Paparoa Range is a unique geological cocktail of sedimentary, metamorphic and igneous rock, and only here and in Fiordland do the mountains meet the sea so abruptly. In fact, 25 million years ago the Paparoa Range was part of Fiordland—prior to splitting away and being carried almost 450 km (280 miles) to the north by the Alpine Fault. There is an added twist—a literal twist—in the form of the Paparoa syncline, a down-warping of the earth's crust to form a trough-like structure which buried much of the region's limestone, preserving it from erosion. This limestone—both the crowd-pleasing pancake rocks at Dolomite

Right Freshwater stream entering the surf of the Tasman Sea, near Gentle Annie Rocks.

Point, and the less well known inland karst—is the geological signature of Paparoa National Park.

The karst is an erratic and secretive landscape, particularly because here, like nowhere else in the country, it is hidden under a thick growth of native lowland forest. Fallen tree trunks bridge limestone chasms, choking deep shafts and sinkholes. The walls of some canyons are fluted into organ pipes so large you can hide inside every groove. A fleece of moss covers everything, and silvery droplets of water streak though it all, chiming and tapping on fern leaves, drip-feeding the underground rivers.

The sinkholes and canyons often lead into caves whose names—Armageddon, Babylon, Xanadu—conjure up images of Gothic interiors, amaranthine beauty and ghostly secrets. The largest of the caves, Metro, named after the Parisian subway, is over 8 km (5 miles) long, a labyrinth of tubular passages with chambers the size of concert halls, lit by constellations of glow-worms.

At one time these caves would have been completely filled with water—part of a subterranean plumbing system for the mountains and forests above. The symmetry and size of their passages speak both of the vast amounts of rainwater they have drained and the aeons over which it has been happening. Dripping, trickling, chiming, roaring, the underground water tirelessly wears away obstacles, imperceptibly altering the caves' shape with the years. Sometimes the flow pauses to gather itself in lakes so still they, too, seem made of stone.

Water adorns what it creates, the delicacy of its handiwork a stark contrast to its rock-dissolving power. With the regularity of pendulum clocks, beads of water drip from roofs and arches, leaving thin rings of crystallised calcium carbonate around the drip zone—like the salt residues left by evaporating seawater. With time, the stacked-up rings form hollow tubes called soda straws. These eventually disappear under new growth and become stalactites. The water dripping from their tips releases still more calcium carbonate as it hits the floor directly below, forming stalagmites, sometimes mirror images of the stalactites above. This process, repeated in its infinite variations, can produce an exquisite cave décor of formations as fragile as spun glass or as solid as the columns of the Parthenon.

Such treasures are well-guarded, not by some mythical underground beast but by the very architecture of the caves themselves. When the water comes across an obstacle it cannot dissolve or otherwise wear out, it finds its way around it, in the process creating spiralling wormholes and 'squeezes' that can trigger a bout of claustrophobia even in the most stout-hearted of visitors.

I experienced just one such secret trapdoor in a cave on the northern fringe of the park. It was like a one-way entry valve into the cave—easy to get down, well-nigh impossible to get back through, for it required an extended bout of wriggling through a long keyhole-shaped opening in the ceiling. My guide weaselled his way up with a mixture of brute force and uneasy contortions. There was much panting and grunting as his gumbooted feet violently scrambled for purchase high above my head. I could hear the rasping of his cordura caving suit against the rock—like a snake, he was using the friction of his 'skin' against the rock to stop himself from sliding back down. Minutes passed, then I heard his muffled voice: 'I'm through. Come on up.'

I made a couple of metres of upward progress, then the walls seemed to seize my upper body with the firmness of a hydraulic press. My feet dangled in the air and I could no longer turn my head, as my helmet had become wedged as well. I stopped to assess the situation, recalling, with rising panic, an incident in which another caver got so severely stuck in a squeeze it took nineteen hours of drilling and chiselling to get her out.

'Undo your helmet buckle,' my guide advised. 'Breath out, then push your chest through one rib at a time.' I did. Five centimetres . . . ten . . . twenty . . . . Slowly the jaws of the vice relaxed and I was through. I stood in the sunlight, gasping. Looking down at the wormhole, nursing the mild aftershocks of panic, I thought, No way do I go down there again. Not for an hour or two, anyway. The beauty I had witnessed in the cave—the crystal flowers that glistened as if made of diamonds—was exquisite and alluring. The price of admission was high, but it was also fair.

Above Pancake Rocks of limestone, Punakaiki.

For all its attractions, until the early 1980s the Paparoas remained relatively unknown. A handful of local cavers had been exploring the area for about a decade, but kept their findings to themselves, and the few hunters and mountaineers who also ventured here liked the place the way it was—close by yet little known, the kind of place that preserves itself through its own rugged topography.

Then Andy Dennis, a scholar with a penchant for translating Icelandic sagas, resigned from his post as a law lecturer at the University of Canterbury and moved to Westport, from where he began systematically exploring the Paparoa Range. The result of four months of field work was *The Paparoas Guide*, the first and definitive run-down of the area's features and attractions. 'It's a biological treasure house,' wrote Dennis, 'a lowland rainforest that is increasingly rare in this country.' In 1987, in recognition of these values, Paparoa National Park was created to protect the largest complete sea-to-mountaintops ecosystem remaining in New Zealand.

Today, despite its growing popularity, the park still guards its many secrets. Away from the coast there are relatively few short tracks, and the amenities are sparse. There is only one longer tramp, the two-day Inland Pack Track, which was once an alternative to the tortuous coastal route and whose main attractions are the aptly-named Ballroom Overhang and numerous small creeks velveted with moss. There is also the Croesus Track which, though outside the Park's boundaries, offers the only easy access to the Paparoa Range tops. It was put into heavy use when the coal miners from Blackball came to Barrytown for Saturday night dances, running—*running!*—over the top of 1220-m (4000-ft) Mt Ryall. The Department of Conservation brochure promotes this walk as a 10-hour overnighter, but, as one Blackball resident told me, 'a fit man could do it in two-and-a-half hours'.

On a crisp autumn afternoon I climb up towards Mt Ryall, then veer off the track and walk for another two hours along the open tops. On the edge of the treeline I hunker down for a damp bivouac, hoping to glimpse, or at least hear, another one of the Paparoas' secrets. I have brought with me a plastic shepherd's whistle, and after darkness has set in I put it to my lips. The first few calls are misshaped and off-key, but then I find the right sound. *Crrweeee! Crrweeee! Crrweeee!* I repeat several times. I pause for a few minutes, then call again. And again. I'm hoping to draw out one of New Zealand's most elusive creatures, the great spotted kiwi. Paparoa and Kahurangi National Park are their most important bastions.

The trick with the whistle was shown to me by ecologist John McLennan, who for many years led the effort to protect these eccentric birds. It relies on challenging the territorial aggression of the bird, posing as another kiwi invading its turf. 'They can fight like devils,' McLennan said. 'Put two estranged kiwi together and soon you may have only one, and a pile of feathers.' Their combat is a furious kick-and-tear kind of karate, with high jumps and lightning-fast blows of sickle claws. Most disputes, however, are resolved through vocal duels.

Suddenly there is a shrill reply to my whistles, the sound of rustling through the tussocks and another penetrating call, so close it makes me want to plug up my ears. I don't have McLennan's night-vision binoculars on this occasion, but I know what the attacker looks like. A shaggy pear-shaped fur-ball propelled by large T-rex feet, sniffing and snorting like an agitated hound, it is surprisingly small for the amount of noise it's making.

I stop whistling in order not to aggravate the bird any further. Quietly I'm proud of it, of its reaction, of its being here at all. Against all odds, the great spotted kiwi is holding its ground. In this harsh environment these birds have out-toughed the predators. And they take no nonsense from an intruder, whatever its size. I hold stone-still against the fur-ball's scrutiny, and after a moment, reassured of its dominance, it relaxes, for I hear it walking away. A rustle in the tussock is followed by the sharp angry sneeze the birds use to blow dirt out of their nostrils, which invariably reinforces their reputation for territoriality and a short-fuse temper. The sound trails off down the mountain. Rustle … rustle … snort!—off goes the kiwi, the ghost of the Paparoa forest.

Opposite Blowholes in limestone gorges near Pancake Rocks at the edge of the Tasman Sea, Dolomite Point.

Above Breakers from the Tasman
Sea roll in on Dolomite Point.
Right Ferns frame the view of the
Dolomite Point surf.

Paparoa National Park

Above Pororari River flowing
through lowland forest.
Left Limestone landforms along the
Pororari River Track.

New Zealand's newest national park embraces most of the country's 'third island'—
diminutive Stewart Island/Rakiura, a place of wild winds, deserted beaches and the
haunting calls of the kiwi.

Rakiura National Park
Beachcombing and bushcrashing Carl Walrond

In March 1890 a ship was wrecked off South Red Head Point, on Stewart Island's desolate west coast. Hammered by a gale, the barque *Emilie* had drifted for five days. Then her mast snapped, cleaving the lifeboat in two. Twelve seamen were aboard. Four survived the ordeal; the sea swallowed the balance. The survivors eked out seven days on the rocks, subsisting on seaweed, woodhens, mussels and a dead seal. Muttonbirders on the nearby Titi Islands sighted the wreckage and rescued the survivors. At any other time of year there would have been no one harvesting muttonbirds, and the castaways would have had to bushcrash their way to the sealers' cave at Doughboy Bay, 12 km (7.5 miles) to the north.

The cave lies behind the dunes, sheltered from the worst of the weather. Sealers with try-pots, clubs and lances once occupied this spot, and the rendering stench of marine mammals filled the air. Now, over a century later, it is I who sit in this fissure in the granite. Bits of planking and fishing net have been fashioned into three crude beds. There is a cupboard set into a crevice, and even a book for people to record their visits and intentions. The soot-blackened walls are marked with carved initials. Who has sheltered within these walls?

Out on the beach, I sit on a driftwood log. The tang of the sea comes to me in waves, strong and metallic, mingling with the smell of dead kelp. It has taken me eight hours to walk here. The mud that coats my legs is flecked with pepper-coloured sand. There is a deep pleasure in knowing that I am the only one in the bay.

I pass up a night in the cave with the rats and the damp for the bunks and potbelly stove of Doughboy Bay's bivouac, a wood and polythene structure built onto a tiny tin hut. A possum tries on three occasions to join me. Pulling aside the black plastic with its paw, it makes its way arrogantly into the shelter. I throw bits of firewood at the animal, and after the third projectile it leaves and doesn't return.

The calls of the local kiwi population fade with dawn, along with my dreams. I drag myself from the fug of my sleeping bag. Outside the hut the ground is pocked with holes, as if someone has been jabbing a stick into the earth. The kiwi have been busy in the night.

I walk the track to the beach. Someone has made a flotsam-jetsam man. The eyes are plastic bottle tops, the arms are bull kelp, the yellow wrap of hair is nylon rope, unraveled into its fibres. The mix of natural and manmade seems an unholy alliance, but somehow it works. This place feels so primordial, so removed from the developed world, but the refuse that fetches up on the beach suggests otherwise.

I comb the beach for a time, then find myself walking back through the dunes to the cave. In 1978 a light plane landed on this beach, bringing four passengers. One was Keiko Agatsuma. She was returning under police escort—to collect some buried money, she said. She had lived here in Doughboy cave, cooking her meals under a rough corrugated-iron barrel. To her this place was the antithesis of her life in Tokyo, where she worked as a cleaner in glass-and-concrete tower blocks. She said she hadn't known places like this existed.

Right Granite archway along the shores of Shipbuilders Cove.

Her visa allowed her 30 days in the country; she took 180 more before New Zealand immigration officials extradited her.

I had read her story in old newspapers. Her intent was to get south, as far south as she could. Australia wasn't far enough. Getting away from Tokyo, that was the important thing. Her family felt like strangers, she said. I thought about her lugging her belongings over Adams Hill, the high point between Doughboy and Mason Bays. Did she have a suitcase? Or did she somehow strap them to her back? How did she cope with the peat bogs, the roots of the bog pine, the steep inclines? When Keiko returned, an odd drama played out near the crest. She led her escort into the forest to look for the money, but nothing was found. The police suspected it was a ruse, a chance to have one last look at the island.

I walk through the bush to a point at the south end of Doughboy Bay. Below me, a seal barks from a gulch and waves suckle the small caves. The track is a mire. The teteaweka—muttonbird scrub—is in flower. It has white petals, serrated leaves and purple-black buds. Rainbows wax and wane. Wavy froth lines stream off the point in the lee of the westerly, and the sun catches the sienna of the taller dunes south of Doughboy Creek. I spend hours trying to catch fish off the point. I hook them readily enough, but their strength exceeds that of my line and they escape my ravenous gaze in silvery flashes. Keiko, I think, would have fished here.

Dumpling-like figures have been hewn out of the headland by the Roaring Forties. The bay is named after these granitoid rocks. Doughboy—an American term. I somehow connect with these strange shapes, carved by the sea's raw breath.

The Piper is late picking me up. The pilot says hunters delayed him at Mason Bay. As we lift off from the beach I see the last images Keiko saw of the island: the blue-black ocean, the forest blanket, the sickle of beach.

Five years pass, and Rakiura calls me again. The plane flies over Mason Bay—a scanning pass. The beach is clear. We bounce along the sand, the motor splutters out. I have sat cramped between two packs for 20 minutes. Through a small rear portal have come images: the swash of waves in Foveaux Strait, the cliffs of the Ruggedy Range, vegetation clinging to rock, just beyond the sea's spray. My knees have locked, and I stumble on to the beach like an arthritic goat.

I pitch my tent on the banks of Duck Creek. In the evening I find a stonefield in the dunes and comb it for ventifacts – stones shaped by wind-blown sand. I take one up in my palm, rub its smooth, pitted facets and run a finger along a distinct ridge. Dust-laden winds have blasted this stone into a pyramid shape. Sand grains have lodged in little surface depressions and whirled around, enlarging them into pits.

Morning finds me at Big Sandhill, where winds have strafed the rock into fan shapes. I descend the dune to the Island Hill homestead, now a Department of Conservation field centre. Introduced grasses and clover grow freely. A gooseberry bush is blanketed with bracken. Dog kennels lie rotting and rusting beneath the macrocarpas. There's nobody here, so I peer through the windows. I see an old cast-iron bath with eagle-foot claws. Beach pumice sits in the soap holder. The window ledges have a layer of dead flies. I make out a wooden washing rack, a green candle in a scallop shell. Out front an aeroplane-shaped wind vane points south-west, its propeller clanging.

There were two sheep runs here in the 1870s. Wool-laden boats crashed out through the surf to waiting ships. In the 1920s a dray road was hacked out of the scrub to Freshwater River, at the head of Paterson Inlet, to get the wool out. In later years the clip was flown out from an airstrip, the aviation fuel costing a little less than what the fleece fetched at sale.

Tim Te Aika, a Chatham Islander, and his wife, Ngaire, farmed the Island Hill run for 20 years. I talked to them near Manapouri, where they had retired. Had any unusual things washed up, I asked? 'An amazing creature—a giant squid between Wreck and Cavalier Creeks,' Tim said. 'I measured it. It was 25 feet long. The body itself was eight feet. The suction cups were one-and-a-half inches in diameter. It made me wonder about

Above Weather-worn granite opening on Bald Cone with the granite domes of Fraser Peaks gracing the skyline, Port Pegasus.

Above Morning shadows linger on the beach in Kaipipi Bay, Paterson Inlet.

the old tales of sperm whales with suction-cup marks a foot across. How big were the squid to have cups that size? I cut the beak out and gave it to the Half Moon Bay School. It was like a parrot's.'

Tim knew where the local kiwi nested. The family used to watch them from the front porch of the homestead. Now that the sheep have gone, the grass is tall and hides the kiwi well. They are comical figures, almost absurd. 'All arse and beak,' a hunter quips in Mason Bay hut that night. I see them shuffling about outside the hut. On the beach, too, foraging for sandhoppers and other comestibles.

The following day I walk to the north end of the beach. Kelp thrashes in the surf. At the far end of the bay a track sign points upwards. 'Little Hellfire,' it reads. The next beach is Big Hellfire. Damnation by degrees.

I find many things cast up by the sea: a bottle of Johnnie Walker Red Label—the label gone but the top still screwed on, divers' flippers, a gas bottle, a dead seagull. Wood sticks out of a peat layer in the sand cliffs. I break off a piece and bite into it—salty and desiccated, it must be circa 10,000 years old. Bluebottles pop underfoot as I walk. At dusk, looking along the curve of the beach, I watch the spray drifting inland, a shroud on the dunes.

In the morning I shoulder my pack and push on south to Doughboy. In the dark forest, yellow lichen flashes from rimu bark like lightning seen through closed eyelids. Red rata flowers litter the track, but kidney ferns are ashen. It has not rained in a while.

Dropping down to the coast I reacquaint myself with bog holes. Sand washes on to the mud, forming a thin layer. It looks firm, but a curse slips out when your foot doesn't do as expected. It is disconcerting. You are never sure whether you will plunge to thigh depth or walk on.

On the rocks, sunburnt kelp crunches under my feet. Low tides and persistent summer easterlies have exposed the seaweed and flattened the sea. I catch a trumpeter off the point and eat some raw sashimi. The olive oil and lemons I have been carrying are not wasted. The hut book describes the rescue of a seal snagged in kelp. The rescuers used knives and a bag placed over the seal's head—'both on long sticks.' It seemed to have worked; the seal was last seen swimming out to sea.

The plane is late again. I comb the beach once more, finding a pilot whale's skull and a dead albatross. Native parrots chatter, flies buzz, seagulls screech. When you are waiting for a plane your sense of hearing is heightened. I hear many false planes. The surf and wind conspire to make engine noises. I wait. The tide has turned. I am resigned to spending Christmas Eve at Doughboy Bay when I hear a true engine.

We bank away, and again I see Keiko's last view of brown-stained river, riffled sand, lapping sea and a beach littered with logs, bones and plastic. It is easy to think of this coast as a graveyard for the Southern Ocean, but flotsam and jetsam—the dead, worn out, bashed over and cast up—is just the visible part of what we can't see in that great unknown, the ocean.

In the Doughboy bivouac I had read in a months-old newspaper that Mugabe's tyranny had exiled a Zimbabwean printer to Christchurch. He said he was happy for now, but his long-term hope was to return. 'Africa is in me,' he said. Some places get under your skin, and once therein you can't shake them loose. Rakiura is like that. In 1986, after 20 years of farming, Tim and Ngaire Te Aika left Mason Bay. But there have been many return journeys. As he said to me, 'We seem not to be over it yet.'

Above Vegetation clings to granite
boulders in Pegasus Passage,
Pikihatati.
Above right Sunset over Paterson
Inlet from Observation Rock,
near Oban.

Above and right Strange granite
sculptures on Bald Cone, Pegasus
Wilderness Area.

New Zealand's first (and the world's fourth) national park preserves a cluster of volcanoes in the central North Island that were gifted to the nation by the paramount chief Te Heuheu Tukino IV in 1887. Tongariro, Ruapehu and Ngauruhoe are some of the most visited, most revered peaks in the country.

Tongariro National Park
Te Heuheu's gift Geoff Chapple

The plan was to tramp the Tongariro Crossing with my wife, but when I rang the Department of Conservation office at Whakapapa, the skifield village on the western flank of Mt Ruapehu, the forecast was forbidding.

'There's snow down to 1500 metres, south-west winds between 75 and 90 kilometres an hour—gale force,' said the woman from the department. 'Stay off the track, it's dangerous. I've already had one group call in by cell-phone from near Red Crater. They've abandoned the crossing. They're coming back.'

'What if we walk up to Ketetahi Hut, overnight there and try for the crossing tomorrow?'

'Okay, you're coming from the northern side. You'll be in bush, then you'll be on exposed mountain-side for an hour. The wind will try to blow you off the track, but it'll be uncomfortable rather than dangerous.'

'And tomorrow?'

'It could be clear in the morning—then we've got more high winds coming in.'

I went across to Troutski's café and store, bought a woollen hat and, in hope of glaring snow the following day, sunglasses. Brent Mander had written the same weather forecast on his notice-board.

'It's not looking good,' he said.

'We'll go anyway—as far as Ketetahi tonight, then hope.'

Mander took me across to an aerial photo of the national park's three big mountains. Tongariro's truncated bulk stood in the foreground, and the store-owner showed me where the route went through.

'I hope you're sure about what you're getting into. Mountain weather is changeable anywhere in the world, and the weather on these mountains even more so. Just over here is the sea, and that maritime climate makes the mountains doubly unpredictable.'

One of the newspaper clips on his notice-board was a *Wanganui Chronicle* item on a 1992 death on the mountain. A fit Turkish-German 21-year-old had gone up Tongariro too lightly clad and simply froze to death.

'Once you get onto the track, don't be afraid to turn back,' said Mander. 'Thousands of people do this walk, but I don't like the word walk. It's a hike. It's great—but you have to respect it. And stay warm. Hypothermia—by the time you start getting woozy it's because the brain is shutting down from lack of blood. At that stage your friends can save you. If you're on your own, tough, you may not even know what's happening. I'm told they found one fatality with his head and shoulders in his pack. Scrabbling to get his warm clothes out.'

It was mid-afternoon when Miriam and I set out. We wound through the lower reaches of the old volcano in bush, and got our first whiff of sulphur from the Mangatipua Stream. At just over 1000 m (3279 ft) the track emerged onto tussock and the knock-down wind.

A driving hail rattled on our hoods. Drifts of the stuff, no bigger than hundreds and thousands, piled up around the tussock. Then it changed to snow. We staggered in the gusts, but kept a good pace and reached the faintly roaring cleft of Ketetahi springs just as daylight began to fade.

Right Mount Ruapehu above Wairere Stream on the Upper Taranaki Falls Track.

We got up before sunrise. Ketetahi Springs was churning beyond the ridge and sending up wild streamers of steam. The air smelled of sulphur, and from this vantage looking north, the land below stretched away to the horizon dark and rumpled, with inset mirrors—the lakes of Taupo and Rotoaira.

We watched the lower territories gradually light up. We ate rice risotto on the verandah. We talked to a pipit on the railing. My God, we were happy as fools! The man from the Department of Conservation, Bruce Ferguson, wrote the weather forecast on the board. Clear through the morning, closing down in the afternoon. The predicted window of blue sky was moving through right on time.

The trail zigzagged up from the hut through intricate pillows of mountain vegetation: gentians, hare-bells, snowberries, mountain daisies, lichens. Then the flora gave out and we climbed on bare rock and ash.

Tongariro is the ravaged old giant of the national park with six craters and one volcanic cleft. As befits the compensations of age, it has accumulated the most jewelry. Blue Lake Crater, for starters. Blue, round, and looking distinctly semi-precious, set there amidst its circle of ice-encrusted rocks. Down, then across the dun-coloured Central Crater, a slug of old lava surged halfway across it. On to the emerald lakes, the first and smallest of them frozen over and purely green. Fumaroles sent up clouds of steam from the shoreline of the largest lake, but it was edged with ice. My intrepid wife decided nonetheless to take a dip.

I sat eating dead-cold bits of chocolate and watched a stream of trampers coming through from the Mangatepopo Hut side. They were taking photographs, eating muesli bars, staring down at the views, and the clear mountain air was freighted with foreign accents. Above us, more people poured two by two over the summit of Red Crater. It was rush hour on the Tongariro Crossing. Animated long johns strode past, their primary banded colours matching the purity of the emerald lakes, the red crater, the blue lake.

And then, as suddenly, they disappeared. I looked north, and a big bank of cloud rose over the ridge.

Miriam dressed, and we slogged up the side of Red Crater. With the eerie swiftness of mountain weather, the clouds rolled in, and by the time we'd climbed up onto Red Summit, there was nothing to photograph but my own Brocken spectre—my enormously magnified shadow cast on a bank of cloud.

We came to a signposted junction. That way down to the Mangatepopo Hut. This way up to a second mountain top. The mist was thick now, and the junction had elements of a dream. The pale wooden sign said 'Ngauruhoe Summit: Two Hours'. What summit? The poled route stretched away into blankness. As I watched, a load of ice slipped off the sign and burst on the ground. Miriam and I walked down the old lava flow to the Mangatepopo Valley.

I tried later to deduce why people flock to the Tongariro Crossing. Partly, it is because the mountain's great clarity simply encases you, like a block of glass. You feel bulletproof, yet you also know it is a trap.

The subdued violence of it is a separate thing. The fissures billow and reek. You can hear the water boiling underground, and if you sit on those sulphur-stained rocks the steam washes over you, scalding hot and then, with a waft of air, freezing cold with the condensate. It is pole to pole extreme.

A few days afterwards I was in a room in the Whakapapa Skotel, putting on all the warm clothes I had. Kieran McKay, an instructor at the Sir Edmund Hillary Outdoor Pursuits Centre, had offered to climb Ruapehu with me—at night, in the dead of winter. McKay brought extra climbing gear for me. The leather lace-up inners and stiff plastic outers of climbing boots. Woollen mitts. Crampons. An ice axe. A hard hat.

We togged up and drove to the ski-field car park. Sodium lights cast an orange glow across Happy Valley, the big snow-groomer garages there, the après-ski café and the first-aid room. The place was deserted. Security lights winked under the eaves. Below, the cloud lay in a quilt that half-encircled Ngauruhoe and edged up to within a kilometre of Ruapehu. The cold air flowing off the bigger peak was keeping it at bay.

It was 9 pm. The moon was high up, a waxing gibbous that cast a ghostly light on the white ridges above. This was a different mountain. Not the Ruapehu of the rough and rocky volcanic flanks, but an aloof Ruapehu

Above Whakapapanui Stream and Mount Ruapehu.

that had drawn a cold white cloak around itself, distilled from winter air. The mountain began to seem less benign. Out to the left were the Pinnacles, where an avalanche had buried two climbers just over a year ago. We kicked footholds in crisp snow, going up the lee side of Knoll Ridge, close to its rounded top.

Over the top, and we were into a 25-knot wind that cast stinging ice particles into your face. On this side, the ridge was coated with thin ice. I'd done some climbing before, but I was no expert, and I simply followed McKay's lead, stamping through the crust with the hard boots.

The ice had thickened slightly. I stamped and transferred weight, but my boot skidded sideways and I slid down the slope a metre or two before stopping myself, stretched full length, one woollen mitt clamped onto a nearby rock with the tenacity of a starfish. McKay turned to watch me lever myself carefully to my feet.

'It might be time for the crampons,' I said.

We put the crampons on and unstrapped the ice axes. We came up to a rock overhang buttressed by snow that sloped down to a short wall of ice. McKay went across and I waited. This was still elementary climbing but, for the first time, it was what they call technical.

We came up to the region dubbed Restful Rocks. McKay called a halt and we sat down in the lee of a rock clump hung with icicles. He broke out hot Milo and peanut-buttered crispbread. We sucked from the water-bottles too, now no longer a liquid but an icy sludge. We were very high, and it was very cold. I'd sweltered under six layers of clothing up to now, but noted my body temperature had now sunk to neutral. Cloud still covered much of the land below, but the lights of Taupo were clear out to the north-east.

McKay looked around and he was happy. 'Incredible, isn't it? To be completely out on your own while the rest of the world is asleep. Just you and a moonlit wilderness.'

Just after midnight we reached a dip in the Summit Ridge, the Notch. For hours I'd been looking up and suddenly I was looking down. The ridge fell away steeply to the summit plateau. The moon was sinking behind us now, bright enough to cast shadows, and two dark figures stood on the white floor 40 m (131 ft) below. They moved when we moved, waved when we waved.

We looked around a huge moonlit amphitheatre. The summit ridge curved away into the left-hand distance, and Ruapehu's northern-most peak rose there off the plateau floor a kilometre or so away—Te Heuheu, squat, powerful, black-slabbed. A more slender and precipitous formation reared straight up from the flat snow directly opposite—Cathedral Rocks, frosted, and steep, and very tall for something that seemed made only of a luminous dust. To the right stood a big white hump, the Dome.

'Surreal eh?' said McKay. 'Like being on the moon, but a bit more wind.'

We went down the ridge towards the plateau, headed south in deep crunching snow, then came up to another ice wall, higher than the last. We swung the ice axes in an arc, embedded the long stainless steel spikes into the rounded top of it, hauled upwards, kicked inwards, and ascended on the cantilevered platforms made by our own boots.

We climbed on towards the Dome.

I had one ambition on Ruapehu—to get to the Dome and look down on Crater Lake. I'd seen pictures of it all my life, pleasantly strange, a big green pond, gently steaming, set into white downs of snow.

Not at all. It was a volcanic throat. If you wanted to see Dante's innermost stone circle of hell, it was embedded right down there in the moonlight. I saw only half the lake, the undulating snows of the Dome foreground hid the rest. I didn't have any desire to go closer. I didn't even want—as they say—to soak up this scene. Maybe it was the time of night, but I found it frightening and I turned away. We sat in the lee of Dome Shelter and sipped more of the Milo, then it was time to go down.

Left Waitonga Falls in the Ohakune Mountain Reserve below Mount Ruapehu.

Above Mount Ngauruhoe and
tussock grasses.
Above right Rangipo Desert with
Mount Ruapehu under clouds.

Above **Lower Tama Lake and Mount
Ruapehu from the Tama Saddle.**
Left **Upper Tama Lake and the
symmetrical cone of Mount Ngauruhoe.**

The North Island's largest national park, Te Urewera, sprawls over crumpled, broken terrain. Its great forests have long been a refuge for birds, plants and people.

Te Urewera National Park

Heart of the fish Shaun Barnett

I quietly shut the door of the Panekiri Hut and step outside into the cool, grey forest. I'm up before dawn, hopeful as always that sun and cloud will create a magic visual moment. My boots feel for footholds among the tree roots on the ridge track. Silver beech forms a low canopy overhead, a lattice of interconnected branches that in the shadowy light blends one tree with its neighbour. At this altitude the trees are stunted, their moss-encrusted limbs bent at arthritic angles by the rigours of weather and temperature.

Lying near the edge of a long bluff on the southern flanks of Lake Waikaremoana, Panekiri Hut is one of several shelters on the four-day 'Great Walk' that partially circumnavigates the lake. Soon enough I find what I've been looking for—a vantage point on the edge of Panekiri Bluff where the trees have separated sufficiently to allow a glimpse of the lake's waters, some 700 m (2295 ft) below. I wait for the sun to rise.

Waikaremoana means 'sea of dashing waters', and indeed the lake is large enough to become unnavigable when storms whip its surface into a fury. Missionary explorer William Colenso, who visited Waikaremoana during an extensive journey through the North Island in 1841, commented, 'I was often struck with the magnificence of the waves of the lake; these seemed to me to be altogether unlike in grandeur and high broken commotion to anything I had ever observed in those of the sea or ocean.'

Today, however, Waikaremoana remains subdued. The western arm of the lake lies under low cloud, leaving only the eastern reaches exposed. The forested ridges of Te Urewera National Park are obscured; in clearer conditions they would sprawl into the distance, line upon line to the horizon.

Rarely are you unrewarded for the extra effort required to rise before dawn. Just as I'm ready to give up, the sun splinters through a gap in the clouds and briefly illuminates the lake, the cloud and the forest. By some trick of the light the low cloud seems to be flowing, slowly cascading through a confined neck of the lake known as The Narrows to dissolve over its eastern half. It is almost as if the lake is on a tilt, gravity pouring the cloud across its surface like molten, milky glass. Then the sun disappears into the high cloud, the light dulls and the illusion fades.

Aptly enough, the land here did once tilt in this direction. No lake existed at that time, but a river did, flowing eastwards. Then, around 2000 years ago, an earthquake triggered a colossal landslide from the nearby Ngamoko Range, sending millions of tonnes of smoking debris into the valley below. This rubble formed a dam as effective as any concrete, and over time the river banked up to form many-armed Lake Waikaremoana. Eventually forest re-established, softening the lake edges and hiding the scars of the landslide. It is profoundly uplifting to know that such beauty can arise out of such destruction.

Lake Waikareiti—Waikaremoana's smaller neighbour—has similar geological origins, but from a much earlier landslide, some 18,000 years ago. Waikareiti formed in a hollow within the debris, as did a number

Right **Cascade on Aniwaniwa Stream.**

of smaller lakes and tarns. Silt is slowly filling in the shallower of these lakes, allowing vegetation to once more gain hold. Some have already become dried lake beds or shallow mires. At some time in the future, Lake Waikareiti, too, will disappear. Time may heal rifts, but can just as surely erase its more sublime creations.

Waikaremoana and Waikareiti, both accessible from State Highway 38, are the primary destinations for most people who visit Te Urewera National Park. I have paddled around Waikaremoana in a Canadian canoe, tramped around it a couple of times, and wandered the mires and lake edges of Waikareiti. But as delightful as this part of the park is, these lakes do not, for me, embody the essence of Te Urewera.

That essence lies instead to the north and west, in the hills and valleys of the Whakatane, Waimana, Waikare, and Waiau rivers. Here a myriad of confusing catchments divides broken ridges to form as complicated a terrain as occurs anywhere in New Zealand.

Legend has it that when the demi-god Maui fished up Te Ika, the North Island, he commanded his brothers to watch over it while he departed to make an offering to the gods. But the brothers disobeyed him, and instead sought to divide the giant fish among themselves. Still alive, the fish thrashed about, creating the riven mountains that so characterise the spine of the North Island. Te Urewera, some believe, is the heart of Te Ika.

If a fish skeleton forms an apt analogy for the landscape of Te Urewera, then its flesh and scales must be forest. Aside from where there are occasional slips, a few small clearings or the river-beds themselves, forests dominate this landscape with almost claustrophobic intensity. Ubiquitous beech, giant northern rata, dense tawa, and stately rimu, totara and miro. And beneath the canopy, a confusion of luxuriant tree ferns, tangled supplejack and a multitude of leafy shrubs.

Only on Mt Manuoha—at 1392 m (4564 ft) the park's highest point—does altitude fully overcome forest. Even here, only a small patch of sub-alpine scrub exists, with trees never more than a few metres away.

Te Urewera is synonymous with forest—dense, green, expansive forest, the largest unbroken extent remaining in the North Island. This is the sort of country that can readily produce a fear of being lost in the bush. Rivers and ridges run in all directions, and rarely is there a break in the trees or viewpoint substantial enough to ascertain your position. While tracks and huts form a basic network over the area now, it's still easy enough to go astray. It takes time, patience and sound navigational sense to know this country well.

One Maori iwi, Tuhoe, know the landscapes of Te Urewera intimately, and its forests have long offered them refuge—from other iwi, from Pakeha, from change. 'The swift rivers and the canyons are my defences, the huge boulders and rock cliffs are my palisades'—this is how Tuhoe describe their land.

Proudly independent, the tribe defied Pakeha influence for many decades, long after other areas of the North Island were cleared and settled. State Highway 38 did not penetrate the width of Te Urewera until the 1930s, and to this day much of its convoluted length remains unsealed.

During the late 1860s Tuhoe harboured the Maori prophet and rebel Te Kooti, helping him wage a guerrilla campaign against Pakeha settlements at Poverty Bay. For this solidarity they were punished, their crops burnt in scorched-earth retribution for defying the British military. During a two-year campaign over 200 Tuhoe died of starvation, disease and hardship, until in 1871 they gave allegiance to the government.

Tuhoe continued to face hardship in the following decades, especially after the government confiscated much of their land. In this setting another Maori prophet, Rua Kenana, rose from Tuhoe ranks. Concerned at the influence of Pakeha on his people, Rua dreamed of an independent Maori community in Te Urewera.

In the first decade of the twentieth century Rua attracted a band of followers that eventually numbered around 600. Under the shadow of Mt Maungapohatu they cleared forest, farmed sheep and cattle, and practised the Ringatu faith founded by Te Kooti. Despite the movement's peaceful intent, the government viewed any independent Maori settlement as suspicious, and eventually trumped up charges to arrest and imprison Rua in 1916. Although Rua was released two years later, the isolation of the Maungapohatu

Above Looking through the ferns to Lake Waikaremoana and Panekiri Bluff.

settlement and crippling fines from the government eventually spelled its demise. Another chapter of Te Urewera history closed.

Like many rural Maori, modern Tuhoe face poverty and the continuing loss of their people to cities elsewhere in New Zealand. Ruatahuna, the major settlement, remains small, and few permanent residents now live at Maungapohatu. Although their way of life in the mountains and their cultural traditions have dwindled along with the population decline, the association of Tuhoe with Te Urewera remains strong. Tuhoe still ride horses through the forests, catch eels in the rivers and hunt pigs among the bracken. Many pockets of land along the major valleys remain privately owned, and some, like Tawhana in the Waimana Valley, are farmed. More recently, some Tuhoe have started small enterprises taking tourists on horse treks and marae stays.

It is perhaps for their horsemanship that Tuhoe are best known. Horses remain a part of life in Te Urewera that is unique among New Zealand national parks. A skilled rider can negotiate many of the larger valleys on horseback, although the narrower, gorged streams remain impenetrable except to those on foot.

Once, while tramping the Six Foot track in the Waimana Valley, I came across three Tuhoe on horseback. Rolled blankets and leather saddlebags lay strapped to the horses' flanks, and the breath of the animals steamed in the chill winter air. Save for my own bright, modern gear, we could have been in the nineteenth century. 'Seen any pigs, bro?' they asked. 'No. Where are you headed?' I asked in return. 'Maungapohatu. We're going back there to stay for a while.' Back to the sanctum, the spiritual centre of Te Urewera.

Northern Te Urewera is a refuge not just for people, but for endangered endemic birds. Te Urewera holds the largest remaining population of kokako, a steel-grey bird of the crow family with tear-shaped blue wattles. Their lineage is old, and includes one other extinct species, the huia, and another, tieke, which is now found only on predator-free islands. Kokako have a haunting melody that seems to speak of such loss.

Another large bird, the kaka, a bush parrot, also finds a stronghold in Te Urewera. Often in the evenings you can hear kaka calling their harsh croaks as they fly above the forest. Kaka once provided a traditional source of food for Tuhoe. Using a captive decoy bird tethered in a clearing, a skilled hunter could catch dozens of kaka by luring them down from tall trees into hidden snares. Steamed in an earth oven or preserved in their own fat, kaka formed an important delicacy and were second only to the kereru (native pigeon) in their importance as food.

The extent of Te Urewera's forests partially accounts for good populations of these and other birds, now rare or vanished from most other parts of the North Island. No matter how large the refuge, though, native birds face a predatory onslaught for which evolution has not prepared them. The Department of Conservation, assisted by the local community, has in recent years established the Northern Te Urewera Ecosystem Restoration Project, an ambitious predator-control programme which tips the survival odds in favour of the birds.

Over the years I have become a 'regular' in these forests, wandering its trails, watching out for rare birds, chancing into new valleys, opening the door of huts that have not seen anyone for months. But why this place in particular? There are other forests with distinctive wildlife, impressive trees and enchanting rivers. Te Urewera does not embody the spectacular country one associates with most other New Zealand national parks. Nowhere are there grand mountains shouldering into the sky, or alpine meadows choked with flowers, or volcanic calderas filled with emerald water.

Here beauty lies in the details. A collection of moss-fringed boulders through which a rippling stream winds its course. A northern rata in flower, splashing the khaki of the forest canopy with brilliant red. A perfectly shaped kidney fern frond, with veins exposed by backlit sun.

Tuhoe have a proverb: 'Return to the mountains that you may be cleansed by the winds of Tawhirimatea.' Perhaps it is this human element that I find most compelling about Te Urewera. The knowledge that others have walked and lived in these forests, finding within them refuge and respite from the outside world.

Left Eastern shores of Lake Waikaremoana.

Above Mosses and lichen drape the
branches of rimu and tawa in the
forest of Te Urewera.
Right Beautiful fern forest surrounds
the walk along the Lake Waikareiti
Track.

New Zealand's third-longest river has been a vital waterway for both Maori and Pakeha. In 1986 its importance was recognised when it was enshrined within its own national park.

Whanganui National Park
A river runs through it Vaughan Yarwood

It was mid-afternoon when a friend and I eased our kayaks into the limpid waters of the Ongarue River at a place called Cherry Grove and set off, gliding 100 m (328 ft) or so until we met the more urgent flow of the Whanganui. There the big-muscled river gripped the hulls of our boats and bore us toward the first of 239 rapids that lie between this junction at the town of Taumarunui and the river mouth, 236 km (148 miles) away. We were heading for Pipiriki, four days distant, a journey that would take us into the heart of Whanganui National Park.

Our guidebook bristled with warnings of snags, rock ledges, whirlpools, crosscurrents, boulders and pressure waves. I knew from experience that, despite the river being classified as grade two, hazards were frequent in these upper reaches.

Now, as we shuddered and slewed through Pokaka rapid and Whakatarino and the foaming Towhenua, grazing boulders, graunching over shingle and glimpsing the ghostly flick past of submerged boughs and rocks, we had little time to take in what lay on either bank. Yet, despite the need to concentrate, something in me seemed even now to loosen, to unclench, to begin finding refreshment. It was good to be back on this haunting, charismatic river.

The Whanganui, New Zealand's longest continuously navigable river, starts life as a small stream to the east, on the slopes of Tongariro, one of three big volcanoes that tower over the North Island's central plateau and are protected within Tongariro National Park. From there it drops down to Cherry Grove, at the town of Taumarunui, where it turns south, following a twisting course to the Tasman Sea through one of the country's largest tracts of native forest.

Getting closer to that lush, primeval forest with its steeply folded gorges often cloaked in mist is a big reason for the river's popularity with adventurers today. Ironically, it was as a means of bypassing that same forest that the river had been used by Maori for much of the previous thousand years. Well into European times, taking a canoe up the Whanganui was the only convenient way of getting from the southern coast to the interior.

Maori settlements once dotted the sheltered valleys of the Whanganui and its tributaries, with 20,000 people or more living off fish, crops of sweet potato and the birds brought back by hunting parties. Today the earthworks of pa (fortified villages) can still be seen amid forest regrowth on the sandstone bluffs. Some were virtually impregnable. Tekateka, for example, perched on a narrow isthmus, could be reached only by swaying vine ladders hung from vertical cliffs 100 m (328 ft) above the snaking river. Such fortresses earned the respect of other tribes, who called the area 'the crayfish's lair'.

Near dusk we made for land ourselves, pitching tents on a sandy terrace above the river. The thick slab of sand, left there by floods, was cool and soft. As our driftwood fire crackled and smoked, the cries of paradise

Right Whanganui River from above, in fern forest near Pipiriki.

duck and spur-winged plover reached us across the water. The first stars rolled out, and two cormorants flew a ruler-straight course downstream.

Next morning we eased into the boats again, and vainly tried to discover the secret to stretching the shock-cord hems of our waterproof spray-skirts around our cockpits in less time than it takes a woman to give birth. I'm here to report that it cannot be done in less time. Nor can it be done the first time. Also, once the thing has at last been done and the kayaker looks like a severely challenged hand-puppet, he or she will unfailingly discover that most of the voracious blackflies of the Whanganui have been trapped below decks and, safely screened from interference, are having an unfettered go at the legs.

With an itch to be gone we paddled into the current, entering the vast roadless tracts of the national park, which wraps about the river's waist. Now and then we came across wooden stakes driven into the river gravel, the remains of Maori eel and lamprey weirs that had stood along the banks in favoured spots, handed down from generation to generation. Whanganui eels, it is said, grew to 2 m (6.5 ft) in length and weighed 25 kg (55 lbs) or more. It's not a big step from there to the ferocious taniwha (water spirits) described in Maori narratives, which are said to lurk beneath whirlpools on the river.

My paddling companion may have had some dealings with these taniwha. Over the coming days I grew accustomed to hearing a strangled *Huooaah!*, at which I would look back in time to catch a disorderly mass of boat and paddles and flailing arms spinning in the white foam.

At Maraekowhai, where the Ohura River cascades over its last waterfall and joins the Whanganui, stand two of the most impressive Maori totems on the river, the 'war pole' Rongo niu, and Riri kore, the 'peace pole'. War poles were rallying points for some followers of the Pai Marire religion in the 1860s. Festooned with ribbons, and with wooden arms outstretched, Rongo niu and others like it called to the warriors to drive out the encroaching European settlers. The peace pole, Riri kore, was later put up at Maraekowhai to mark an end to the bloodshed.

Maraekowhai became familiar to people around the world when the entrepreneur Alexander Hatrick launched a shipping venture on the river in the 1890s. With guile, luck and dogged perseverance he forged a passenger and freight service that eventually stretched upriver all the way to Taumarunui, carrying supplies and produce for isolated farms and opening the Whanganui to tourists.

Hatrick used giant paddle steamers on the broad lower reaches, each capable of carrying 400 people. At Maraekowhai, below the Pai Marire poles, he ingeniously moored a custom-made houseboat for his guests. Lavish company advertisements and picturesque postcards extolled the beauty of what was romantically marketed as 'the Rhine of Maoriland', but behind the glamour lay danger and backbreaking work. Men toiled ceaselessly to detonate boulders and clear the river of snags. Beneath fist-sized holes punched in the soft siltstone cliffs by Maori canoe poles can still be seen one of the ring bolts used to laboriously winch Hatrick's boats up through the shallow rapids. Elsewhere, stone groynes still go about the business of channelling the river's flow to scour and deepen the bed.

Victorian travellers may have ridden more impressive boats elsewhere, and on bigger rivers—the Amazon, the Nile and the Yangtze—but nowhere in the world were steamers run under such trying conditions. The Whanganui was a shallow, twisting river, which surged through any number of rapids, was subject to sudden floods and, during the busy season, suffered dramatically reduced flows. One traveller called the experience 'steamboating on a trout brook', while another likened it to 'sliding down a mountain on the dew'.

After a day spent in the thick of history, we landed at Whakahoro, near the mouth of the Retaruke, and caught a lift up to the campsite on the back of a truck. A dead goat lay tied across the hood. 'Dog food,' said the driver. 'Shot it downriver.' Feral goats infest the Whanganui, getting into any place where a cliff offers space for an agile hoof. The goats persist despite forest-protection programmes that kill them and the equally

Above Dense foliage surrounds a narrow chasm, near Pipiriki.

destructive possums in their hundreds. At stake is the forest canopy and the native birds that depend on it.

We ate by torchlight on the grass plateau surrounded by bush-clad hills. Overhead the Southern Cross shone with cold brilliance from a clear sky. Dawn, however, brought rain, which soon grew to a thunderous downpour, driving us from the leaky tent to the camp hut, a former country schoolhouse, and its blazing woodfire. There, a retired teacher turned novelist and volunteer hut warden, Sid Hill, set aside his oboe and filled our day with cider and stories of medieval England. He was an unlikely find in such a wilderness.

Next morning we packed our blackflies and again hit the river, astounded at how far the Retaruke had risen—almost 2 m (6.5 ft). It was furiously pumping muddy water into the Whanganui, staining it the colour of strong tea for kilometres. Dogged by rain and low cloud, we pressed on through the river's middle reaches, where forested cliffs thick with scarlet-flowered rata trees twisted ahead of us. The local population of long-tailed cuckoos had quit the Whanganui to overwinter in the Pacific Islands, but herons lingered, and now and then the pure notes of a bellbird bounced off the water. Once, a violent crack split the silence as a forest giant lost its footing and toppled down the face of a cliff, its crown smashing theatrically into the current.

We passed Tarepokiore, a whirlpool so strong that before being tamed by blasting it could spin riverboats around, and Oparia rapid, where a 100-warrior canoe, the giant Tauwharepuru, used to be lowered from the clifftop on supplejack ropes. Afternoon brought us to a new Department of Conservation hut on a bend in the river. A 40-minute climb up the steep wooded ridges behind the hut, bordering what our map soberly labelled a 'remote experience zone', brought a view of valleys and unbroken forest to the south.

Back at the hut, a gibbous moon rose through the branches of a tree where a colony of rare long-tailed bats roosted. Despite a setting worthy of Dracula, no bats appeared, though the constelled light of glow-worms shone from damp fern-covered banks overhanging the path.

Next day we stopped briefly at what turned out to be a deserted village. Climbing a path beneath supplejack arches we came to a silent courtyard overhung by karaka trees. Steam rose off the compacted earth, and washing hung limply from a makeshift line. The sun caught a Maori sovereignty flag pinned under an awning. Birdsong drifted in the still air.

We pressed on to Tieke marae. Tieke had been the site of a Department of Conservation hut until one day in 1993 Maori arrived by jetboat and began a peaceful occupation, reclaiming the land that had slipped from tribal ownership early last century. It is now a place where wayward young Maori come for time-out and to be taught something of their culture.

Our arrival stopped a volleyball game up on the grass terrace. Francis, a young Maori, picked his way down to the shingle to help us with our gear. After a formal welcome, we stepped into a dirt-floored dining area roofed by a canvas tarpaulin. Here, by the glow of an open fire, we ate and drank and swapped yarns. After the evening meal, Francis, who can trace his ancestry back for 24 generations, told something of the history of the place. In time past it was an important trading hub on the river. A carved meeting house once stood nearby. Francis pointed to the spot. Behind screens put up to protect it from the gaze of the women, a carved totara pole now lay. When finished, this pou whenua or land pole, would stand as a marker of belonging.

Next morning, as we prepared to leave, I mentioned to Francis that we had visited the upriver settlement and found no one. He smiled. The people were on a pilgrimage, he said, taking the spirit of a dead relative down the river, stopping at places along its course that were special to him.

Memories are long on this river.

As we pushed off for Pipiriki, I lifted a hand to Francis, who stood alone on the shingle bank, his figure dissolving into the thick cloak of forest. Ahead lay more picture-postcard scenery, splendid caves and the metre-high pressure wave of Autapu rapid.

Huooaah!

Left Fern forest alongside the Whanganui River.

Above Tree ferns at forest edge,
Whanganui River Canyon.
Above right Whanganui River
Canyon in the rain.

Joined at the spine with Mt Cook National Park along the mountainous Main Divide, Westland National Park boasts 60 named glaciers nestled within 87,000 hectares of rugged hinterland. Two of them, Fox and Franz Josef, are among the country's premier tourist attractions.

Westland National Park
The ice kingdom Derek Grzelewski

Discovery can be a haphazard affair. Although the glittering peaks of New Zealand's Southern Alps were noted by Abel Tasman and James Cook as they sailed along the South Island's west coast in the seventeenth and eighteenth centuries, the region's two signature glaciers, Fox and Franz Josef, were not mentioned in European records until the vessel *Mary Louisa* passed by in 1859. An entry in the ship's log reads: 'We saw what appeared to be a streak of mist running from between two peaks ... At noon, abreast Mount Cook, close inshore, we could see distinctly that it [probably Franz Josef] was an immense field of ice, entirely filling up the valley.'

Franz Josef was known to Maori as Ka Roimata o Hinehukatere, 'the tears of the avalanche girl'. According to legend, Hinehukatere, a Maori woman who often ventured into the entrancing world of towering mountains and shining snowfields, persuaded her lover, Tawe, to accompany her on one of these escapades. As they climbed near the great peaks of the Main Divide, Tawe, lacking confidence in this unforgiving terrain, slipped and plunged to his death. Hinehukatere wept with grief, and her endless tears were frozen by the condoling gods into a stream of ice.

In 1864, Julius von Haast, the Prussian-born provincial geologist of Canterbury, visited the glacier and prosaically dubbed it Franz Josef after the Austro-Hungarian emperor.

At that time, the glacier's terminus pressed hard against Sentinel Rock, a 282-m (925 ft) outcrop known as a *roche moutonnée*, which had survived the onslaughts of previous glaciations. For most of the following hundred years, despite several minor re-advances, the snout of the glacier receded some 3 km (1.9 miles). Then, in 1983, a year with a markedly El Niño weather pattern, the recession stopped and the glacier started advancing rapidly. A small retreat followed around the turn of the century, but now the glacier is on the march again.

When I first visited Franz Josef Glacier, in 1993, its snout was 15 m (49 ft) short of the viewing gallery, a wooden barrier perched on ice-polished rock. A looming wall of bulging, broken-up ice—characteristic of advancing glaciers—hung over the valley floor. Long ice pinnacles, reaching the crest of the wall, toppled over like soldiers in a firing line. It was a spectacle of crushed ice, falling rocks and burbling water accompanied by groans and grunts from the bowels of the icy beast.

Several weeks later, the snout reached the rock, pushed against it, stopped temporarily, and began building up in height and volume. The viewing gallery had to be moved 70 m (230 ft) downhill; the glacier was reclaiming its ancient territory.

The névés of Franz Josef and Fox Glaciers have one of the highest precipitation levels in the world. Annual rainfall can be as much as 15 m (49 ft) in this region, and in the mountains 1 m (3 ¼ ft) of rain equates to about 3 m (about 10 ft) of snow. This, coupled with the fact that the valleys on the western side of the Divide

Right Morning reflections, Lake Matheson. Tucked under the clouds are Mounts Tasman and Aoraki/Mount Cook.

are narrow and steep, means that these glaciers move like greased lightning compared with most—as much as 7 m (23 ft) a day. And what makes them even more special is that they descend to just 200 m (656 ft) above sea level; frozen waterfalls flanked by luxuriant forest.

Occasionally, Franz Josef has been a troublesome neighbour for the small community that lives in its valley. In 1965, after heavy rainfall, the glacier became so saturated with water that its snout burst like an overpressurised dam. Ice and rock shrapnel showered the valley and the neighbouring forest. The unleashed river surged towards the sea, carrying chunks of ice that were still 50 cm (20 in) across when they met the foamy West Coast breakers some 20 km (12.5 miles) away.

During a similar event in 1991, the collapsing terminal face sent a tsunami-like shock-wave sweeping along the valley. The bridge over the main coast road survived the onslaught, but it was yet another reminder to the residents of Franz Josef not to take their glacier for granted.

Long-time glacier guide Peter McCormack showed me where hanging galleries were once strung across the smooth rock slabs in the never-ending battle for tourist access to the ice. Today they have all rotted away. Only ochre-brown patches of rust around the weathered bolts recall the engineering ingenuity of long ago.

'This track here used to be a road.' Peter pointed at a path that cuts through a gorge made of house-size rocks. 'In the 1950s we could drive right up to the snout. Now the road is under 30 feet [9 m] of gravel.'

Among the floods and avalanches caused by the glacier, one has been welcomed—the flood of tourists. Nowhere else in the world are the advancing glaciers as easily accessible as on the West Coast, and as the word has spread, Fox and Franz Josef have turned into bustling boom towns. Their main streets have all but disappeared behind a facade of billboards advertising glacier tours, scenic flights, restaurants, motels and shops. A helicopter pilot can clock up 30 flights on a long summer day; he leaves the engine idling even during refuelling.

Such bustle and commerce would have astonished—and probably dismayed—the legendary nineteenth-century explorer and surveyor Charlie 'Mr Explorer' Douglas, who spent almost four decades roaming the gorges and glaciers of Westland at a time when big chunks of that territory were still a blank. In the 1860s, a journey from Christchurch to Hokitika via Arthur's Pass took five days of hard travelling, and south of Ross there was only a rough coastal track cleaved by wild, unbridged rivers. The latter claimed so many lives that drowning was considered a natural cause of death.

Douglas was a nomad and a loner, travelling light and living largely off the land while making geological observations, survey notes and sketches. Pipe, dog and solitude were his chief companions. His shelter was a floorless A-shaped tent fashioned out of two sheets of calico, yet this tiny bedroom gave out onto the largest living room of all: the wilds of Westland. Here he thrived and felt at ease.

'Fools say that knowledge can only be acquired from books & men,' he wrote in his diary in 1902. '[They] call me a fool & even worse for wasting my life in mountain solitude, simply because I don't open up mines of gold & silver. I have now been wandering about the uninhabited parts of New Zealand for over five & thirty years, always finding something in nature new to me and the world ... glimmerings of truth unknown to others.'

Often I have tried to put myself in the waterlogged boots of this enigmatic explorer, eager to learn from his experiences of a lifetime spent in the wilderness. With his diaries for a guide, I have criss-crossed Westland National Park and its neighbouring terrain, paying my way in blood extracted by the West Coast's vampiric sandflies. Sometimes I hitched a ride with a bush plane. More often I paddled a canoe, grateful for an easy passage in the tangled forest. But mostly I travelled on foot. Looking and listening and staying quiet, I hoped to get a glimpse of Charlie's world and to see what was out there to fill such a restless lifetime, what riches he had found.

Above Peaks of the Southern Alps in the alpine light.

There is perhaps no better way to experience Douglas country than by tramping the Copland Pass, a trans-alpine route from Mt Cook to the West Coast. The crossing, usually done in the east–west direction, requires rudimentary mountaineering skills. Basic alpine gear—ice-axe, crampons and rope—is essential, and the assistance of a mountain guide is advised. But don't let that deter you, for when you stand at the notch that Copland Pass makes in the spine of the Southern Alps and look down and to the west, taking in Copland Glacier and the valley wending down between the Sierra and the Navigator Ranges, you are seeing the very essence of Westland National Park.

The landscape seems compressed, the space between its glaciers and the sea squeezed like a concertina. At your feet, the scree slopes—sterile and seemingly devoid of life—plummet sharply into the valley, but as you begin the descent the transition from alpine barrenness to rainforest lushness is so astonishingly fast it seems as if the vegetation is rolling up to meet you.

The trail is a botanist's delight, and a feast for all senses. Just below the snowline, among the moonscape of rock and scree, the first lichens and mosses appear, then the sprawling cushion plants—'vegetable sheep' and forget-me-nots—which soften the contours of stones, muffling the sounds made by footsteps and the tendrils of running water.

Moments later you see edelweiss, delicate as snowflakes, and white and yellow buttercups, bright as miniature suns, their hardy leaves often rolled cup-like, dewed and half-filled with rainwater.

Another sharp drop in altitude along the zigzagging trail and you are walking through alpine meadows among mountain daisies and willow herbs, all soft and luxuriant, and almost blindingly green after the black-and-white world of snow and rock.

Shrubs appear: coprosma, hebe and tree daisies, mountain wineberry and holly. Then suddenly the trail flattens and you enter the beech forest, shady and cool, a home to shy deer, cunning weka and the gluttonous native pigeons. These last routinely gorge themselves on berries until they are almost too heavy to fly. When startled, they launch themselves into a desperate nose-dive glide and crash-land in a nearby tree.

At the end of a long and intense day's tramp you arrive at a hut named Douglas Rock after a nearby shelter Charlie Douglas used during his time here. Further down awaits Welcome Flat, with its set of natural hot pools, which soak out the exhaustion from bones and muscles while offering a stunning view—the serrated skyline of the Sierra Range.

The descent from Copland Pass into the Westland rainforest has always seemed to me like a journey into life itself, from austerity at the beginning of things to the lushness of the many-branched Darwinian tree; a walk through the evolution of plants where the sequence is played on fast-forward.

In an oblique sort of way, it was Charlie Douglas who inspired me so see Westland in this way. I have grown affectionate of his unseen but influential presence, and during my adventures in the national park I've come to treat him as an absent friend, an old forest pundit always willing to share his experience. His diaries make a thoughtful and entertaining guidebook, for he was an avid connoisseur and collector of those rare moments in the wilderness when the senses sharpen and we look at the world with the eyes and the heart of a poet.

For him the Westland wilderness may have been small in size but it was vast in detail, a perfect place to try to grasp William Blake's 'world in a grain of sand, And a heaven in a wildflower.' For Douglas, Westland *was* that world, and he explored it with intense passion, not for credit or glory or material reward, but for the knowledge itself, the understanding born of nature and silence.

Left Franz Josef Glacier from Sentinel Rock.

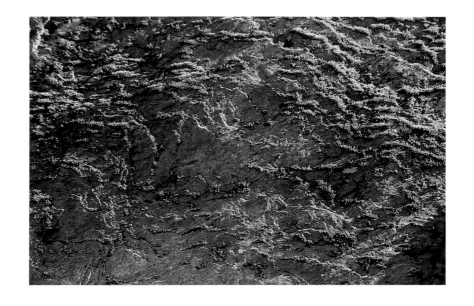

Left **Fox Glacier in the rain.**
Right **Detail of moss on rock near snout of Fox Glacier; lichen and moss; mountain daisy.**

Above Serrated skyline and
steep broken face typical of the
Southern Alps.
Right The magnificent Fox
Glacier, the largest and longest
of the West Coast glaciers.

Above Sculpted rock gives a
sense of the movement and
enormity of scale of Franz Josef
Glacier, as it grinds its way down
the mountain.
Left Ice window in the Franz
Josef Glacier.

Visitor Information

Te Urewera National Park

Gazetted: 1954.

Location: Between the Bay of Plenty and Hawke's Bay in the North Island. The nearest towns are Whakatane and Taneatua to the north, Murupara and Ruatahuna to the west, and Wairoa to the east.

Size: The largest national park in the North Island and the fourth largest in New Zealand, it covers 2,126 sq km (821 sq miles). The land rises to 1,400 m (4,593 ft), forming part of a mountainous spine running from East Cape to Wellington. Lake Waikaremoana, at the centre of the park, is 550 sq m (5,920 sq ft).

Features: The most extensive forested wilderness remaining in the North Island. There are more than 650 species of native plant. The vegetation pattern is not static; over the years volcanic activity, fire and storms have all left their mark. Much of the park is remote and not easily accessible. This has helped to protect some of the park's native wildlife and it is home to kiwi, kaka, falcon and the distinctive whio or blue duck.

Activities: The park's many tracks includes the Lake Waikaremoana Track, one of New Zealand's Great Walks. Huts are situated along the 46 km (28.5 miles) of track; most can also be accessed by boat. Shorter walks are also available, including one to Lake Waikareiti. Boating and fishing are popular on Lake Waikaremoana. Brown and rainbow trout are found in the lake.

Facilities: There are numerous backcountry huts in the park, ranging from basic to those with more facilities on the Lake Track. A Great Walks Pass is required for huts on the Lake Track.

Whanganui National Park

Gazetted: 1986.

Location: Between Mt Taranaki (Egmont National Park) to the west and Mt Ruapehu (Tongariro National Park) to the east, with the township of Taumarunui to the north and Wanganui to the south. The small towns of Pipiriki, Ohinepane, and Whakahoro are the main gateways to the river itself.

Size: 742 sq km (1,286 sq miles) in three sections of the scenic high points of the Whanganui River. The Whanganui River—the second longest in the North Island at 329 km (204 miles)—rises on Mt Tongariro and winds in a long south-westerly curve through the central volcanic plateau to the Tasman Sea near the city of Wanganui.

Lowland forest surrounds the river in its middle and lower reaches – the heart of Whanganui National Park. The water body and bed of the Whanganui River are not included in the national park.

Features: The Whanganui is canoeable for over 200 km (124 miles) and it was an important transport route for Maori over many hundreds of years, and for the early European settlers. Erosion has created spectacular gorges, bluffs and a maze of intricate ridges and V-shaped valleys. The waters are an important habitat for the whio or blue duck, an endemic torrent duck.

Activities: The Matemateaonga Track, one of two major tracks in the park, is one of the most remote tramps in the North Island. This four-day track follows old Maori tracks and a graded settlers' road across the crests of the Matemateaonga Range. Transport by jetboat is needed to or from the river end of the track. Jetboating itself is a popular river pursuit.

Facilities: The trip down the Whanganui is classified as a Great Journey and a pass is required from October to April to use the facilities on the river. It is a relatively easy river to canoe or kayak and is suitable for novices. There are huts and campsites along its banks.

Tongariro National Park

Gazetted: 1894.

Location: Central North Island. The nearest towns are Turangi (around 6 hours' drive from either Auckland or Wellington), National Park and Ohakune.

Size: 796 sq km (307 sq miles), and includes within its boundaries Ruapehu, Ngauruhoe and Tongariro, the three major active volcanoes in the centre of the North Island. Tongariro, at 1,968 m (6,456 ft), is the lowest of the three.

SOUTH ISLAND

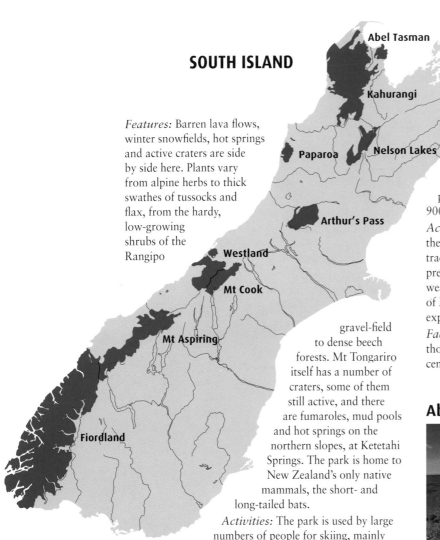

Features: Barren lava flows, winter snowfields, hot springs and active craters are side by side here. Plants vary from alpine herbs to thick swathes of tussocks and flax, from the hardy, low-growing shrubs of the Rangipo gravel-field to dense beech forests. Mt Tongariro itself has a number of craters, some of them still active, and there are fumaroles, mud pools and hot springs on the northern slopes, at Ketetahi Springs. The park is home to New Zealand's only native mammals, the short- and long-tailed bats.

Activities: The park is used by large numbers of people for skiing, mainly on the slopes of Mt Ruapehu, on the ski fields of Whakapapa and Turoa. For trampers, there are many easy, short walks. The traverse of Mount Tongariro (known as the Tongariro Crossing) is a one-day walk. It can be done as part of the longer Tongariro Northern Circuit, one of New Zealand's Great Walks.

Facilities: There are backcountry huts throughout the park, linked by track systems. From October to June, a Great Walks Pass is required for the four huts on the Tongariro Northern Circuit.

Egmont National Park

Gazetted: 1900.

Location: Taranaki, on the west coast of the North Island. New Plymouth, Inglewood, Stratford and Opunake are all within easy driving distance, with good road access. There are three roads entering the park and visitors can drive to a height of 900 m (2,953 ft) on each one.

Size: 335.3 sq km (129.5 sq miles) of native bush and more than 145 km (90 miles) of tracks and routes.

Features: The dominating feature of this park is Mt Taranaki (also called Mt Egmont). The area's high rainfall and mild coastal climate has allowed a lush rainforest to develop, covering 90 per cent of the park. There are also many waterfalls within the park, one of the most popular being Dawson Falls, 900 m (2,952 ft) up the south-eastern side of the mountain.

Activities: A variety of easy, short walks branch off the main access roads and a well-defined tramping track circles the mountain. All visitors should be well prepared as Egmont is particularly susceptible to rapid weather changes. The best time to climb to the summit of Mt Taranaki is January to April. This is suitable for experienced trampers/climbers only.

Facilities: There are camping facilities and cabins for those attempting the climb to the summit. There are visitor centres at both North Egmont and Dawson Falls.

Abel Tasman National Park

Gazetted: 1942.

Location: Top of the South Island. The nearest towns are Motueka, Takaka and Kaiteriteri.

Size: At 225.3 sq km (187 sq miles) the park is New Zealand's smallest, yet the most visited. It rises to a maximum altitude of 1,156 m (3,792 ft).

Features: The park is most noted for its golden sandy beaches, the unspoilt river estuaries, and its intriguing landscape constructed from granite, limestone and marble. The interior of the park is riddled with caves, most notably Harwood Hole, the deepest sinkhole in New Zealand at 357 m (1,171 ft). The more common forest birds, like tui and bellbirds, can be seen around the estuaries and wetlands.

Although the park's boundary excludes the estuaries and seabed, the Tonga Island Marine Reserve was created along part of the Abel Tasman coast in 1993.

Activities: The Abel Tasman Coast Track is one of New Zealand's most popular walks. It is an easy 3- to 5-day tramp on a well-serviced, well-marked route. The track follows a coastal route, with many sections being affected by the tide, particularly at Awaroa where it crosses the wide bay. The inland track takes you through the hilly centre of the park. Sea kayaking and boating rival tramping as popular pursuits in the park.

Facilities: There are four huts along the Coast Track and four inland. There are also 20 campsites with water supply and toilets. Huts and campsites must be booked all year round. The Coast Track is a Great Walk, requiring Great Walk passes.

Kahurangi National Park

Gazetted: 1996.

Location: In the north-west corner of the South Island, due west of Abel Tasman National Park. The nearest towns are Motueka, Takaka, Karamea and Murchison.

Size: At 4,520 sq km (1,745 sq miles), this is New Zealand's second largest national park. The highest point is Mt Snowden at 1,856 m (6,089 ft).

Features: The park contains some of the world's deepest caves, including both limestone and marble bluffs, arches and sinkholes. New Zealand's oldest fossil was found here. An incredible variety of fauna and flora includes more than half of the country's native plant species and about 100 native bird species.

Activities: Kahurangi has a range of walking tracks that vary from easy to very challenging. The Tasman Wilderness Area, which is untracked and without huts, is recommended for experienced trampers only.

The most popular track is the Heaphy Track, one of New Zealand's Great Walks. The Wangapeka Track is also very popular, and there are many short walks close to the roads. The Karamea River runs through the park, and canoeing, rafting and kayaking are popular. Rafting tours are also available. The river is also popular for trout fishing and recreational hunters stalk the many deer and goats, in season.

Facilities: There are huts and campsites along the Heaphy Track. Because of the track's popularity, a hut or camp pass must be purchased from a DOC office to walk along the track and there is a two-night limit at any hut.

Nelson Lakes National Park

Gazetted: 1956.

Location: in the north of the South Island; it surrounds lakes Rotoiti and Rotoroa—the sources of the Buller River—in the northernmost reaches of the Southern Alps. The gateway to the park is St Arnaud, 1.5 hours' drive from Nelson or Blenheim.

Size: 1,020 sq km (394 sq miles). The original park covered 575 sq km (222 sq miles) hectares (142,097 acres) and was expanded to its present size during the 1980s. The land is broken and mountainous with peaks rising to 2,200 m (7,217 ft) from dense beech forests.

Features: The bushline, where forest gives way to alpine plants, is a remarkable feature of the park; the change is abrupt and uniform as if drawn with a ruler. A highlight of the park is the Rotoiti Nature Recovery Project, 8.25 sq km (3.2 sq miles) of land that has been set aside as a mainland refuge for the recovery and re-introduction of native species within a pest-free environment. Bird species include tomtits, robins, the tiny rifleman and the South Island kaka.

Activities: Skiing (in the Mt Robert area), tramping, hunting and trout fishing are the major recreations of the area. There are good winter climbing routes suitable for experienced trampers and climbers.

Facilities: There are a number of backcountry huts in the park linked by a network of tracks. St Arnaud and Lake Rotoroa have camping grounds.

Paparoa National Park

Gazetted: 1987.

Location: On the West Coast of the South Island between Westport and Greymouth, alongside scenic State Highway 6.

Size: This is one of New Zealand's smaller parks at 3,056 sq km (118 sq miles), but includes a variety of environments and some stunning landscapes, perhaps most famously the Pancake Rocks at Punakaiki. The park's boundaries were carefully chosen, not just to protect the area's forests and minerals, but also a full range of ecosystems from mountains to coast.

Features: Visitors encounter high sculptured mountain ridges, impressive river canyons, delicate cave formations and the distinctive plate-like coastal formations. Limestone, the bedrock beneath most of the park, is responsible for these landforms. Waves have pounded through the limestone in places to create blowholes which, when the tide is right, perform spectacularly. Much of the lowland area inland is covered in rain forest, while glades of nikau palms give the forest a subtropical feel.

Activities: Though much of the park is wild and untracked, there are some easy coastal walks along with some to the more accessible limestone features in the park. One of the most popular is the Inland Pack Track, which dates back to gold-rush days. Other activities in the park include canoeing, rock-climbing and caving.

Facilities: DOC has a visitor centre at Dolomite Point.

Arthur's Pass National Park

Gazetted: 1929.

Location: Three hours northwest of Christchurch, straddling the Southern Alps. The very scenic State Highway 73 runs through the park and through Arthur's Pass village, the gateway to the surrounding area.

Size: The 9,927-sq-km (3,834 sq mile) park is mountainous, ranging in altitude from 245 m (904 ft) at the Taramakau River to 2,408 m (7,900 ft) at Mt Murchison.

Features: There are divergent habitats on either side of the main divide. To the east, mountain beech/tawhai predominates; while the west features rata and mixed podocarp rainforest. Kea, the alpine parrots, may be encountered.

Activities: Walkers are catered to with short walks into the alpine zone and day walks to the summits of the surrounding mountains. For overnight hikes, there are tracks and routes leading to more remote spots. There is also a range of climbing options, including Mt Rolleston, a good climb for novices at 2,275 m (7,464 ft).

Facilities: Over 30 backcountry huts and shelters are scattered within the park, linked by a network of tracks and routes. A DOC camping area is located in Arthur's Pass village and there are basic camping facilities at most main entry points into the park.

Westland National Park

Gazetted: 1960. Part of the Te Wahipounamu South-West New Zealand World Heritage Area.

Location: South Westland, about halfway down the West Coast of the South Island. State Highway 6, between Hokitika and Haast, is the only road to the park. While it shares its eastern boundary with Aoraki Mt Cook National Park, this park could not be more different, situated as it is on the 'wet side' of the Southern Alps. Westland contains the greatest diversity of vegetation and wildlife in the New Zealand national parks system. The small centres of Weheka/Fox Glacier and Waiau/Franz Josef are on the park boundary. Hokitika, 2 hours to the north, is the nearest town.

Size: 1,275 sq km (492.5 sq miles) of rugged mountain landscape, dense forest and fast-flowing rivers.

Features: To the east of the Alpine Fault the Southern Alps rise suddenly, their steep slopes heavily forested. High above, permanent snowfields feed a number of glaciers, including Fox and Franz Josef Glaciers. Dense rain forest covers the lowlands west of the Fault. Nearer the coast, scenic lakes, wetlands and wide river mouths feature.

Activities: There are short walks to the terminal face of the two famous glaciers. Guided walks onto the glaciers are available, as are scenic flights over the glaciers and alpine snowfields. The high peaks of the park are suitable for experienced mountaineers only.

Facilities: Five huts in the park cater specifically for mountaineers and ski-tours, and six backcountry huts cater for walkers. There is a visitor centre in Waiau/Franz Josef village.

Mt Cook National Park

Gazetted: 1953, part of the Te Wahipounamu South-West New Zealand World Heritage Area.

Location: The park headquarters are near the famous Hermitage Hotel in Mt Cook village, 747 m (2,450 ft) above sea level. The village, which is served by an airfield, is 338 km (210 miles) south-west of Christchurch (about five hours' drive away).

Size: This 706.9 sq km (1,273 sq mile) park shares a common boundary with Westland National Park. Within its boundaries are the highest mountains and longest glacier in New Zealand and Australia. Nineteen peaks rise to more than 3,000 m (9,842 ft) above sea level. The highest, Aoraki/Mt Cook itself, is 3754 m (12,316 ft). Glaciers cover 40 per cent of the park's area.

Features: The park has virtually no forest, but it is alive with alpine plants. Birdlife is restricted to species that like an open habitat, most notably the kea, pipit, rifleman, bellbird, and grey warbler. The braided riverbeds of the area are home to the black stilt, one of New Zealand's and the world's rarest birds.

Activities: Walkers can choose from ten short or day walks around Aoraki/Mt Cook village and into the Hooker and Tasman Valleys. For experienced alpine trampers there are two alpine routes – over the Copland and Ball Passes. Regular scenic flights take visitors among the high peaks and over the Tasman Glacier. Guided ski trips suitable for intermediate skiers can be taken down the glacier. Helicopters can take experienced skiers into more remote loctions.

Facilities: There are 17 huts in the park, most are located for mountaineering use and require climbing skills to reach them. The park also contains one camping area.

Mt Aspiring National Park

Gazetted: 1964.
Part of the Te Wahipounamu South-West New Zealand World Heritage Area, along with Aoraki/Mt Cook National Park, Westland National Park and Fiordland National Park.

Location: Straddles the southern end of the Southern Alps, stretching south from the Haast River to the Humboldt Mountains, where it borders Fiordland National Park. The closest towns are Wanaka, Queenstown and Te Anau.

Size: 3555 sq km (1,372 sq miles), New Zealand's third-largest national park.

Features: Mount Aspiring, from which the park derives its name, is the only peak over 3,000 m (9,842 ft) outside Mount Cook National Park. The park has forests, native tussock and glaciated alpine country. Beech forests dominate the bushline, and above are snow tussock grasslands and herb-fields.

Activities: The park contains several good walking tracks, including the Routeburn, Greenstone and Caples tracks, the latter two forming a loop walk. The Routeburn is one of New Zealand's Great Walks, and offers an excellent combination of rainforest and sub-alpine environments. The park's alpine areas are suitable only for experienced trampers or mountaineers. Jetboating is popular on the park's larger rivers.

Facilities: A booking system operates for the Routeburn and all accommodation must be pre-arranged. There are numerous backcountry huts and established camping areas on many tracks.

Fiordland National Park

Gazetted: 1952, now part of the Te Wahipounamu South-West New Zealand World Heritage Area, along with Aoraki/Mt Cook National Park, Westland National Park and Mt Aspiring National Park.

Location: Fiordland is the south-western region of the South Island, most of which is covered by the national park. The gateway to the park is Te Anau, 3½ hour south-west of Queenstown.

Size: At 12,523 sq km (4,835 sq miles) this is the largest national park in New Zealand, and one of the largest in the world.

Features: Spectacular fiords, notably Milford Sound and Doubtful Sound, and Lakes Manapouri and Te Anau (the South Island's largest lake), also Sutherland Falls (New Zealand's highest waterfall). Certain areas within the park contain indigenous flora and fauna of such significance that access is by permit only. Other areas have been classified as 'wilderness' (access by foot only), and 'natural environment' (to remain as they are, but with bridges and huts available).

Activities: As well as many short walks, the park contains four of New Zealand's most popular walking tracks: the Routeburn, Hollyford and Kepler Tracks, and the world-famous Milford Track.

Facilities: There are tourist hotels at Manapouri, Te Anau and Milford Sound, and other accommodation, from motels to huts to camping sites, at many places through the park. During summer, advance booking is essential for the three Great Walks tracks (Routeburn, Kepler and Milford).

Rakiura National Park

Gazetted: in 2002.
Location: This park is on Stewart Island, 30 km (19 miles) south-west of Bluff, at the bottom end of the South Island.

Size: 1,570 sq km (1,606 sq miles), about 85 per cent of Stewart Island's land mass. The highest peak is Mt Anglem/Hananui at 980 m (3,215 ft).

Features: The northern half of the island is covered by podocarp and hardwood forest, featuring New Zealand's southernmost tall trees – rimu, kahikatea and totara. There are opporunities to view kiwi in the wild, as some birds feed during daylight hours. Nearby Codfish Island is a pest-free nature reserve, and is now home to the last remaining kakapo that once lived on Stewart Island.

Activities: 245 km (152 miles) of walking tracks can be accessed from Oban, Stewart Island's only settlement.

Most tramping on the island is challenging, not least because of the weather. Trampers should be prepared for wet, windy weather and muddy conditions at any time of year. The popular Rakiura Track, a designated Great Walk, provides a 3-day loop of the island.

Facilities: A Great Walks pass is needed for the Rakiura Track and its huts and camp sites.

Note: We recommend that all visitors to New Zealand's national parks check the Department of Conservation (DOC) website at www.doc.govt.nz for safety tips and further information.